2003
Yearbook

THE YEAR IN REVIEW 2002

People

92
Hollywood's Big Nights

Making room on their mantels in 2002 were Denzel Washington and Halle Berry at the Oscars (left), Jennifer Aniston and the rest of her *Friends* at the Emmys, Alicia Keys at the Grammys and MTV newcomer Avril Lavigne.

104
Tributes

We remember the contributions of Milton Berle (right), Dudley Moore, Britain's Queen Mother, Waylon Jennings, Billy Wilder, Rosemary Clooney, Ted Demme and Jam Master Jay, among many others who left us too soon.

Staff

Editor Elizabeth Sporkin **Senior Editor** Richard Burgheim **Art Director** David Schlow **Associate Editor** Allison Adato **Chief of Reporters** Toby Kahn **Picture Editor** Brian Belovitch **Reporters** Anne Hollister, Michelle Tan **Copy Editor** Tommy Dunne **Operations** Mimi Bessette, Mauricio Vale **Special thanks to:** Brian Anstey, Jane Bealer, Robert Britton, Sal Covarrubias, Urbano DelValle, Laura Downey, Regina Flanagan, Maura Foley, Sally Foster, Margery Frohlinger, Patricia Hustoo, Rina Migliaccio, Maddy Miller, Gregory Monfries, Rashida Morgan, Charles Nelson, Susan Radlauer, Mikema Reape, Annette Rusin, Jack Styczynski, Gail Toivanen, Ann Tortorelli, Randy Vest, Celine Wojtala, Patrick Yang

President Rob Gursha **Vice President, Branded Businesses** David Arfine **Executive Director, Marketing Services** Carol Pittard **Director, Retail & Special Sales** Tom Mifsud **Director of Finance** Tricia Griffin **Marketing Director** Kenneth Maehlum **Assistant Marketing Director** Vanessa Cunningham **Prepress Manager** Emily Rabin **Associate Book Production Manager** Suzanne DeBenedetto **Associate Product Manager** Linda Frisbie **Special thanks to:** Robert Dente, Gina Di Meglio, Anne-Michelle Gallero, Peter Harper, Robert Marasco, Natalie McCrea, Jessica McGrath, Jonathan Polsky, Mary Jane Rigoroso, Steven Sandonato, Bozena Szwagulinski, Niki Whelan

People of the Year

We toasted Nia's Greek wedding, cheered the return of nine brave miners, saw Shakira shake her thing and were moved by Bruce's soundtrack for our times

The Osbournes

MTV'S ANSWER TO OZZIE NELSON, THE HEAVY-METAL PATRIARCH BECAME
A CUDDLY TV DAD, AND HIS LOVABLY PROFANE CLAN AMERICA'S NEW FIRST FAMILY

I DON'T BLOODY UNDERSTAND WHY PEOPLE think it's funny, me taking out the trash," said Ozzy Osbourne. "I mean, I don't have a f---ing trash roadie." That's just part of his surprising charm: He doesn't see the surreal amusement of watching a 54-year-old heavy-metaler struggle with the garbage outside his Beverly Hills mansion. Who knew the man notorious for biting the head off a bat had grown so domesticated? Credit wife Sharon, 50, with saving his life (she helped him control his alcohol and drug use) and repackaging the doom-and-gloom rocker as father of the year. Kids Kelly, 18, and Jack, 17, are as foulmouthed as their folks but obviously two smart, con-fident teens who actually dig their parents. They also became lionized stars in their own right. Jack scouted talent for a record label, and Kelly offered up a respectable version of Madonna's "Papa Don't Preach." (Daughter Aimee, 19, declined to partici-pate.) Despite Ozzy's bemusement, the show is undeniably funny. It's also affecting. Their real life, spilled out in half-hour episodes, had a whole nation pulling for Sharon's quick recovery from colon cancer. And com-miserating and cheering when misfit Ozzy attended a White House dinner. Of his new gig, Ozzy concluded, "I know I'm dys-functional by a long shot. But what guide-lines do we have to go by? *The Waltons*?"

George W. Bush

EMBOLDENED BY A STRONG APPROVAL RATING, THE PRESIDENT FLEXED HIS NEWFOUND POLITICAL MUSCLE AT HOME— AND AGAINST HIS FATHER'S ONETIME FOE

THE YEAR BEGAN AUSPICIOUSLY. HAVING routed the Taliban and battened down the hatches against terrorism, the President now enjoyed an 80-plus percent approval rating. That was comparable only to Ronald Reagan on a good day, so perhaps his nights as a punching bag for comics were behind him. Then in January, while watching football on TV, Bush, 56, inhaled a pretzel and fainted to the floor, monitored only by his dogs, Barney and Spot. (Jay Leno went to town on the incident, prompting Laura Bush, 56, to visit the show and vow that her man would henceforth practice "safe snacks.") The President seemed equally impervious to larger problems, including a stalled economy and a scary stock market. The citizenry saw their life savings hammered—thanks in part to rapacious, unethical CEOs—but didn't seem to blame Bush's pro-business Administration. His media-savvy staff wrapped every policy in a blanket of security and artfully staged the backdrops for his blunt message. At Mount Rushmore, for example, he promised to "hunt the killers down one by one." When Osama bin Laden eluded capture, Bush made Iraq's Saddam Hussein the proximate enemy and asked Congress for carte blanche to take him on. As the November elections neared, even some usually dovish Democrats went along. Pumped by that momentum and pushed by political strategist Karl Rove, the White House homebody stumped tirelessly through 15 states, helping his party to reclaim the Senate and to gain House seats as well. It was the best midterm showing by a President since FDR. Within a week, Bush won again, securing U.N. clearance to retaliate if Iraq obstructed weapons inspections. Once mocked as an insular Texan and lightweight leader, the President was now challenging to become the heavyweight champion of the world.

Rosie O'Donnell

SHORN OF HER TV SHOW, HER
MAGAZINE AND MUCH OF HER HAIR,
SHE BEGAN LIFE ANEW—AND OUT

SHE INSISTED THAT HER CRUSH ON Tom Cruise was real. "I never once said I want him naked in the bed. I want him to mow my lawn and get me a lemonade," she told Diane Sawyer, who had asked O'Donnell, 40, how to reconcile her oft-discussed crush with the revelation in her memoir, *Find Me,* that she is a lesbian. Soon after, O'Donnell gave up her talk show of six years, telling fans that she wanted more time with her three kids and partner Kelli Carpenter, 35, a former TV exec (who was shortly pregnant). Next she sliced into her nice-as-pie image, performing a blue stand-up set at a casino. Then the hair went (inspired, she said, by a Boy George backup singer). Finally she walked away from her magazine, *Rosie.* "If I'm going to have my name on a magazine, it has to be my vision," said O'Donnell, who met her publisher's $100 million lawsuit with a $125 million countersuit. Had she changed, or was this who O'Donnell always was? Whichever, friends stood by, including Cruise, who appeared on her final show pushing a lawn mower and offering lemonade.

Winona Ryder

AT A TRIAL DUBBED 'SAKS, LIES & VIDEOTAPE,' A JURY FOUND THE ACTRESS GUILTY OF SHOPLIFTING

C AN ANYONE SEE MS. RYDER WITH THIS ON TOP OF her head?" Echoing O.J.'s if-the-glove-doesn't-fit-you-must-acquit defense, Ryder's lawyer Mark Geragos (with her, above) asked jurors if it made any sense that the fashionable star would steal a tacky (if $200) hair bow. None of it made any sense. Why would the millionaire two-time Oscar nominee shoplift some $5,500 in merchandise from the Beverly Hills Saks Fifth Avenue after making a $3,000 legitimate purchase? Surely not—as Saks employees said that she'd claimed—to prepare for a sticky-fingered film role. (Her lawyer denies that Ryder mentioned a movie and said she'd believed the store had charged the other items to her credit card.) Could she have been stealing for the rush, as had her character in *Girl, Interrupted*? Motive was indeed hard to establish, but incriminating evidence was abundant. A security videotape made during Ryder's December 2001 spree showed her emerging from a dressing room with one bag fuller than when she entered. Then a store detective testified she saw Ryder snipping off antitheft tags using scissors later found in Ryder's pocket. The actress never took the stand but projected innocence sartorially with shirt-collar dresses and schoolgirl headbands. The display failed to convince a jury of her peers—including Peter Guber, a top honcho at Sony when it released three Ryder films. She was found guilty of grand theft and vandalism. Tabloid headline writers rejoiced. WINONA 'SCISSORHANDS' ENDS HER 'AGE OF INNOCENCE' was among the tantalizing possibilities. Because Ryder had no prior record, the D.A. didn't seek jail time but asked for probation, community service and restitution to Saks. 'LITTLE WOMAN' AVOIDS THE BIG HOUSE.

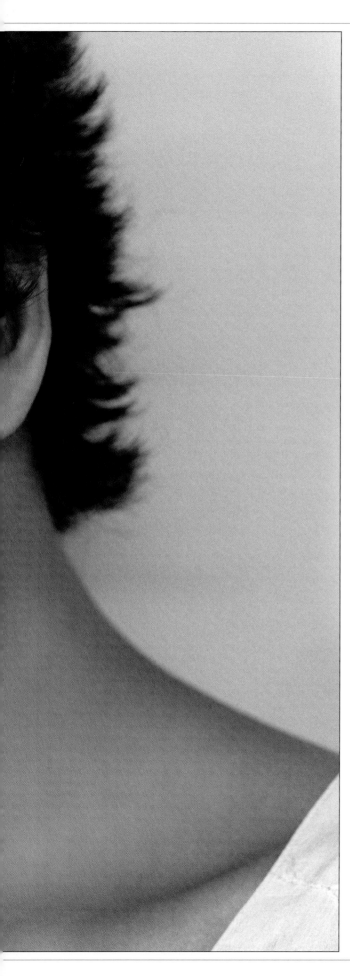

Halle Berry

A PRETTY FACE ONCE OPENED DOORS FOR THE ACTRESS, BUT A GUTSY, UNGLAMOROUS PERFORMANCE HELPED HER MAKE OSCAR HISTORY

THE GOLD STATUETTE WAS ALL HERS, BUT HALLE BERRY was in the mood for sharing. In a tear-streaked speech that made previous podium sobfests look positively dehydrated, the prom-queen-turned-model-turned-actress offered an eloquent acknowledgment that her win, the first for Best Actress by an African-American, belonged to a whole community. "This moment is for Dorothy Dandridge, Lena Horne, Diahann Carroll," said Berry, 36. "It's for the women who stand beside me—Jada Pinkett, Angela Bassett, Vivica Fox. It's for every nameless, faceless woman of color who now has a chance because this door tonight has been opened." Coming down to earth a bit, she thanked her mother, her manager (who, she said, was "the only father I've ever known") and her husband, musician Eric Benét, 36, and stepdaughter India, 10. Having heard her pour out her story to Barbara Walters for a show that aired the same night, the world would understand that this was a personal victory too. Berry had survived a broken home in Cleveland, an acrimonious divorce from base-ball player David Justice and a violent relationship with another man whose blows to her head, she said, left her 80 percent deaf in one ear. A few naysayers sneered that Berry had had to get naked and embody a racial stereotype in *Monster's Ball* to win. Bassett, for one, sniped that "I would love to have an Oscar, but it has to be for something I can sleep with at night." But the vast majority hailed her award, coupled with Denzel Wash-ington's Best Actor victory, as a watershed. Having shown that she is more than a gorgeous face and body, Berry would remind people in her next role, in *Die Another Day,* that she's that too. Smiling, she exulted, "I'm a Bond girl! Classic Bond babe! It's great!"

Bono

THE VETERAN ROCK SINGER LENT HIS VOICE TO THE WORLD'S POOR

HALFTIME ACTS AT THE SUPER BOWL ARE GENERALLY selected to fit comfortably between the cheerleaders and the beer ads. But for the championship game that followed 9/11 by five months, what was called for was a band that could not only rock but also possessed gravitas. Fortunately U2 was free, as its singer Bono had just completed his two-day stint at the World Economic Forum in New York City. Since 1999, Bono (born Paul Hewson), 42, has lobbied the globe's richest nations to forgive the debts of the poorest. A March meeting with President Bush led to a commitment of $5 billion in foreign aid. In May the Irish rocker toured Africa with U.S. Treasury Secretary Paul O'Neill, 67, to convince him of the impact of investment in undeveloped areas. In between, he toured with U2, picked up four Grammys and spent time with his wife of 20 years, Alison, 42. The very vocation of the tireless singer-activist, summed up band manager Paul McGuiness, is to "knock down a lazy thought, whether it's a bad political argument or a mundane lyric."

Saddam Hussein

ON CLOSER INSPECTION, A PICTURE EMERGED OF A TYRANT RULED BY HIS OWN INSECURITIES

ADOPTING AN ARABIC VERSION OF DOLLY PARTON'S "I Will Always Love You" as a campaign song, Iraq's peasant-turned-president carried the 2002 election with a supposed 100 percent of the vote. Half a world away, President Bush, apparently aching to finish the job his father had begun during the 1991 Persian Gulf War, called for "regime change" in Iraq. Encouraged by Defense Secretary Donald Rumsfeld, Bush alluded to links between Iraq and the al-Qaeda terrorists who carried out the September 11 attacks, as well as to Saddam Hussein's purge of more than 100,000 Kurds in the 1980s, some with poison gas. With the carefully negotiated support of the U.N., Bush gave Iraq an ultimatum: Disarm or we're coming to get you. Saddam eventually agreed to open up his 20 palaces and other key locations to inspectors seeking "weapons of mass destruction." Saddam, 65, who seized power in

1979, was raised in rural poverty and beaten brutally by his stepfather. Iraq's "Great Uncle" reportedly has four wives and five children and put two sons-in-law to death for revealing weapons secrets. "He's afraid all the time," said a former security official, and Saddam keeps constantly on the move—with 40 bodyguards, food tasters and at least three doubles to serve as decoys. In mid-October he threw open his jails, freeing tens of thousands of murderers, lesser criminals and political prisoners in a curious act of national reconciliation. Saddam emblazoned "God Is Great" on the Iraqi flag and commissioned a Koran scripted in 36 liters of his own blood. And, perhaps most surprising, he wrote a romance novel which became an epic musical drama. The message of *Zabibah and the King*, wrote a state-run paper, was "to love one's homeland, despite all danger." No hidden message there.

Bruce Springsteen

REUNITED WITH HIS E STREET BAND, THE NEW JERSEY
ROCK POET PENNED A HEALING ALBUM ABOUT THE
TRAGEDY THAT UNFOLDED ACROSS THE HUDSON

TO PUT TOGETHER *THE RISING*, HIS FIRST STUDIO ALBUM
in seven years, Bruce Springsteen reached back
into his catalog of unreleased songs to include a few
poignantly appropriate gems like "My City of Ruins."
It had been written about a hard-luck New Jersey town
but aptly described New York City after September 11,
2001. Writing from the perspectives of the bereaved,
or of a fireman, or of a suicide bomber, Springsteen
came up with no less than a soundtrack for 2002. It was
a year in which America struggled hard to get back to
normal and to not, as speakers often said, let the terrorists
win. At the same time, we all felt an insistent tugging that
something wasn't as it had been. Even those who, like
Springsteen, hadn't suffered a personal loss on 9/11
found their conversations circling back to that day and
to its fallout. As a result, in a cultural climate that made
stars of the Britney-and-Justin generation, the 53-year-
old rocker climbed the charts once again. Suddenly, an
historically media-shy artist seemed to be everywhere at
once. He and Matt Lauer tooled around Asbury Park in
a convertible for the *Today* show. Ted Koppel left the
Nightline studio to interview Springsteen on his farm.
David Letterman had him on two consecutive nights. The
uncharacteristic promotional blitz made even a few fans
flinch. Wasn't it too soon for a pop album based on the
nation's tragedy? Others, like Staccy Farrelly of New
York's Staten Island, came to his defense, saying that
Springsteen's interest in healing was real. Shortly after
9/11 he had phoned her and other widows whose husbands had been identified in their obituaries as Boss fans.
Rather than leave her starstruck, the man who had been
singing about blue-collar workers through three decades
put the fireman's widow at ease. They talked about their
kids—Springsteen's a dad to three preteens—and about
her loss. "After I got off the phone with him," said
Farrelly, 44, "the world just felt a little smaller."

Charles Moose

A MARYLAND COUNTY'S SHY TOP COP ACTED AS A CENTER OF PUBLIC CALM DURING A KILLING STORM

KIDS STOPPED PLAYING OUTSIDE. ADULTS WERE AFRAID to pump gas. People of all ages worried about falling prey to a nameless, faceless, heartless sniper picking off random victims in parking lots and school yards. As the days shortened in September and October, fear chilled the Maryland and Virginia suburbs of Washington, D.C. The man whom residents, indeed the whole nation, looked to for reassurance was Montgomery County, Maryland, police chief Charles Moose. It was he whom the sniper taunted with phone calls and a note scribbled on a tarot card saying "I am God." It was Moose, 49, who was criticized by some experts for fueling the killer's compulsion to manipulate by becoming too emotional in his press conferences. A married father of two with a Ph.D. in urban criminology, Moose teared up after a child was shot. But he moderated his responses, and eventually the sniper was linked to a murder in Alabama, where fingerprints broke the case open. Moose then broadcast a description of the killer's car. Converted into a roving shooting range, it was spotted at a highway rest stop by a trucker who used his rig to block the exit until police arrived. Working in concert with the FBI and police in several other states, Moose's team hauled in the two alleged gunmen, John Muhammad, 41, and Lee Malvo, 17, the son of Muhammad's ex-girlfriend. Ultimately suspected in more than 20 shootings (14 fatal) across the country, the pair would be tried first in Virginia, where prosecutors sought the death penalty. "We have the weapon. It is off the street," Moose announced. Then he added, in one of his last statements before returning to his preferred anonymity, "We have not given in to the terror."

Jennifer Aniston

WHEN SHE LANDED *FRIENDS* EIGHT YEARS AGO, SHE COULDN'T BELIEVE HER LUCK. THEN IT GOT EVEN BETTER

MAYBE SHE WAS MOTHER TERESA IN A previous incarnation. For some, excellent karma is the only explanation for Aniston's blessed life. She was wooed by, then wed to, Brad Pitt, with whom she recently set up house in a $13.5 million Normandy-style mansion in Beverly Hills. She is the It Girl of the It Show of the last decade—and won an Emmy for her efforts in 2002. Then, just when it looked like playing Rachel Green in that show would be the best we could say about her, she went and nailed a funny/sad role in the independent film *The Good Girl,* and critics fell over one another to say that she's not just a Star, she's an Actress. (Even she sometimes can't believe her life. When she got the *Good Girl* script, she wondered if it had been missent to her, the cute girl on *Friends.* She told her agent, "Let's say yes before they realize they've sent it to the wrong person.") *Friends* costar Matthew Perry had another theory: "She's worked hard to put herself in a position to do what she wants to do."

This year the hard work meant carrying the Rachel-has-a-baby story line, making it funny and moving but not in a syrupy way that might make the network want to advertise it with the line "Thursday: A Very Special *Friends.*" The birth on the season finale brought the show its second-highest rating ever and led reporters to turn up the frequency of the question about when Jennifer, 33, and Brad, 39, are going to start a family. Love, career, kids. It seems even as admirers wondered how Aniston came to enjoy such blessings, they wished her only more.

Vin Diesel

IN A STAR-MAKING ACTION VEHICLE, HE BROKE AWAY FROM THE PACK

PEOPLE KEEP ASKING IF I'VE CHANGED SINCE BECOMING A CELEBRITY," SAID Diesel. "I haven't, because I've always thought that I was a celebrity. It was the rest of the world that hadn't figured it out." In 2002 the world got a clue. The self-styled action hero (he dumped his birth name, Mark Vincent, for a moniker that would give him "more confidence") broke out of his supporting role in 2001's money printer *The Fast and the Furious* and returned as the headliner of *XXX*. Commanding an A-list fee of $10 million, Diesel portrayed an extreme-sports-star-turned-spy, a James Bond for a generation raised on PlayStation. (That's probably the same demographic that envies a 35-year-old actor who dates an 18-year-old Czech model.) Raised in New York City's Greenwich Village by an astrologer mom and a drama teacher stepdad, Diesel told his own fortune early on. "I've always been certain," he said, "that I was going to be a movie star."

Hamid Karzai

INTO A VOID OF CHAOS LEFT BY THE TALIBAN, A COSMOPOLITAN LEADER TOOK THE REINS IN AFGHANISTAN

I THINK A WAVE OF PEACE AND UNITY IS COMING TO OUR country," said Karzai, 45, in both Pashto and Dari, as he accepted interim leadership of Afghanistan after its liberation from the Taliban. In June the Indian-educated Pashtun tribesman was elected president of a nation of factious warlords with an economy dependent on smuggling and opium farming. Surviving an assassination attempt, Karzai sometimes even dressed for unity, choosing an Uzbeki robe and a cap from Kabul, prompting Gucci's Tom Ford to call him "the chicest man on the planet." Wed to an M.D., 28, Karzai said of his impossible job: "How do I do this? I don't know. I just go ahead."

Dennis Kozlowski

A GREEDY CEO REDEFINED THE TERM 'PIGGY BANK'

KOZLOWSKI ONCE KNEW THE VALUE OF HARD, HONEST TOIL FOR A BUCK. Waiting tables while attending Seton Hall, he objected to a restaurant policy of pooling tips, preferring to keep what he earned. In those days CEOs got 39 times the pay of their average worker. Now it's 1,000 times, but in a year that saw a handful of CEOs unseated amid scandal, Kozlowski emerged as the most egregious of the greedheads. As chief of Tyco, he took home a $125 million package yet allegedly looted the conglomerate of an additional $135 million for a still more lavish lifestyle. Beach homes in Nantucket, Massachusetts, and Florida. Private plane. Yacht. Birthday fetes with Jimmy Buffett as the entertainment. A Manhattan pad with paintings by Renoir and Monet, a $15,000 dog umbrella stand and a $6,000 shower curtain. Finally tripped up by failing to pay a paltry $1 million in sales tax on the art, Kozlowski was slapped with tax evasion charges by the New York County D.A. His resignation came soon after, and Tyco attempted to collect on the former chief's "loans." But it was too late for employees whose 401(k) accounts dwindled with Tyco's stock price, as investors fled a market rocked by corruption at the top.

Jacqueline Marris & Tamara Brooks

IN A YEAR OF 'AMBER ALERTS,' TWO TEEN STRANGERS KIDNAPPED AT GUNPOINT BECAME FAST ALLIES AND BRAVELY BATTLED FOR THEIR LIVES

QUARTZ HILL, CALIFORNIA, OUTSIDE L.A., IS A PEACEFUL PLACE WHERE local teens hang out. Brooks, 16, was there on a summer night with pal Eric Brown, 18. Marris, 17, was also there with a friend. Close to midnight, Roy Ratliff, 37, a convicted felon wanted on a rape charge, approached Brown's SUV, waving a gun. After kicking Brown out of the vehicle, the gunman forced Marris from her car into the SUV and sped off. By dawn an Amber Alert, meant to notify the public about a child abduction, went out over the media and on highway signs. Meanwhile, Marris and Brooks, who knew Brown kept a knife in the car, devised a plan to free themselves, silently tracing letters on each other's hands to communicate. "He kept telling us he would kill us," recalled Marris (left). "I hoped I wouldn't go to hell for killing him," said Brooks. When Ratliff stopped the car, Marris stabbed him, while Brooks hit him with a bottle. Still, their kidnapper persisted, threatening them with his gun. Tipped off by a motorist who saw the SUV, police quickly arrived, shooting and killing Ratliff. Traumatized but safe, the girls went home soon after. "We were really there for each other," said Marris. "We said, 'I came here with her, and I'm leaving with her.'"

Abducted

ELIZABETH SMART, 14, was taken at gunpoint in June from her Salt Lake City home. Her sister, 9, watched in terror and said nothing for three hours. A suspect, Richard Ricci, 48, died of a brain hemorrhage while in custody on another charge, leaving the family without a lead.

DANIELLE VAN DAM, 7, was snatched on a February night from her San Diego bedroom while her dad and two brothers were at home. A neighbor, engineer David Westerfield, 50, was found guilty of kidnapping and murder.

ASHLEY POND & MIRANDA GADDIS, 12 and 13, who lived in the same Oregon City, Oregon, apartment building, disappeared in similar manner two months apart. Their bodies were later found in the backyard of neighbor Ward Weaver, 39, whose daughter Mallori, 13, was a friend of Pond's until Pond accused Weaver of molesting her in 2001. If convicted, Weaver, whose father is on death row for other murders, could face capital punishment as well.

Avril Lavigne

A SCRAPPY SKATER KID PROVED YOU DON'T HAVE TO STRIP TO BE AN MTV STAR

I DON'T LIKE THAT TERM, 'THE ANTI-BRITNEY.' It's stupid," said the Canadian popster with the hottest debut album of 2002. But in the pigeonholing world of MTV and radio, everyone's got to be something. So if you can captivate the little girls who buy (or burn) CDs without writhing onstage with an albino python, then you're the anti-Britney. And obviously pro-success. Her album *Let Go* went triple platinum on the strength of hooky tunes like "Complicated" and "Sk8er Boi." (Lavigne, 18, raised in the tiny Ontario town of Napanee, is a dedicated skateboarder.) Unlike her peers, Lavigne appears in her videos fully clothed, usually in baggy fatigues, tank tops and a loosely knotted tie. Still, the tomboy attitude and gear may be just as calculated as Britney's sexpot pose. But once girls started coming to her concerts in neckties, the teen star announced she was giving them up. "I get sick of things quick," she said. With luck, her young fans won't.

Simon Cowell

BRUTAL HONESTY—EMPHASIS ON *BRUTAL*—MADE HIM SUMMER TV'S GUY-YOU-LOVE-TO-HATE

T O SAY, 'YOU SUCK, YOU'LL NEVER MAKE IT,' I HAVE a problem with that," griped Paula Abdul. Cowell, who sat on the *American Idol* jury with Abdul, didn't have that problem. In fact, he relished the opportunity to open contestants' eyes to their lack of talent. "Is it more hurtful being cruel to someone when they've sung badly, or giving them false hope?" asked the English record exec. If you agree that it's kinder to be cruel, you might find Cowell, 43, to be a softy. But many of the viewers who tuned in to the surprise summer addiction considered Cowell the unholy spawn of

Ed McMahon on *Star Search* and Triumph the Comic Insult Dog. "If you win this competition, we will have failed," he told one of the contenders for a $1 million recording contract. (Of course, even those voted off benefited from the exposure. Fans expect to hear more from Tamyra Gray, the third runner-up.) But ultimately it was the audience, and not Cowell, who crowned a champ, the peppy Texas cocktail waitress Kelly Clarkson, 20. The show may or may not make her a star. It already has of Cowell, a bachelor who will get $2 million for dishing out a second season of abuse.

Queen Elizabeth II
A ROCK-SOLID MONARCH CELEBRATED 50 YEARS ON THE JOB, WITH NO PLANS TO RETIRE

WHEN THE QUEEN, 76, CELEBRATED HER 50TH year on the throne, her reign had outlasted 10 prime ministers and 30 pet corgis. She had also seen three of her four children through embarrassing divorces. Her upper lip never wavered, but after the 1997 death of Princess Diana, the public cried out for a more emotive monarch. Though never becoming a huggy or chatty woman, she softened some. And the nation did seem to embrace her and revel in jubilee festivities. With her family at her side (including, significantly, Prince Charles's date, Camilla Parker-Bowles), she hosted a Buckingham Palace concert featuring Paul McCartney and Ozzy Osbourne as serenely as if it had been chamber music. As Winston Churchill said of the new Queen in 1953, "If they had scoured the globe, they could not have found anyone so suited to the part."

Cedric the Entertainer
HE GOT FOLKS TALKING, THEN LEFT THEM LAUGHING

ROSA PARKS AIN'T DO NOTHING BUT SIT HER BLACK ASS down," boomed Cedric's curmudgeonly barber. Such cracks in the movie smash *Barbershop* drew disapproval from other characters in the scene—plus protests from two political clerics. Jesse Jackson objected, and Al Sharpton called for cutting the lines from the film. (They weren't.) Cedric, 38, once a St. Louis insurance claims adjuster, just wanted laughs. He got them with less controversy in a new Fox variety show, playing a slew of characters, including a Barry White-inspired therapist. The burly comedian, married with two kids, also does an unlikely song-and-dance routine. "There's a reason they call him Cedric the Entertainer," noted *Barbershop* costar Ice Cube. "He can do it all."

Jake Gyllenhaal

WOOING OLDER WOMEN, A FRESH NEW
LEADING MAN WOWED THE MOVIE CRITICS

HIS FACE SHOULD PLACE HIM IN *TEENBEAT*, but he longs to be on the *Charlie Rose* show. With Tobey Maguire beefing up for action flicks, Hollywood had an opening for a young, thinking brooder. Enter Gyllenhaal, 22, an L.A.-bred showbiz heir (Mom's a screenwriter, Dad's a director). He impressed reviewers with three 2002 pictures. *Lovely & Amazing* (romancing Catherine Keener, 43) and *The Good Girl* (courting Jennifer Aniston, 34) were topped off by *Moonlight Mile,* in which he shared lead billing—and was inevitably compared with—Oscar winners Susan Sarandon and Dustin Hoffman. Not since *The Graduate* had a kid turned a glum, twentysomething role into such a star-making vehicle. (If his unusual surname—it's pronounced Jill-en-hall—seemed ubiquitous in the listings, it was because big sister Maggie, 25, headlined the indie black comedy *Secretary.*) About being the next big thing, Gyllenhaal offered this perspective: "It's like, I've always been a big thing…to my mom."

Denzel Washington

A DECORATED ACTOR CALLED THE SHOTS

"FORTY YEARS I'VE BEEN CHASING SIDNEY. THEY finally give it to me, what'd they do? They give it to him the same night," joked Washington, as he became only the second African-American to win a Best Actor Oscar (for *Training Day*). Earlier that evening, Sidney Poitier, 75, accepted a lifetime achievement honor. At 47, Washington wasn't ready for that, but added, "I'll always be chasing you, Sidney. I'll always be following in your footsteps. There's nothing I would rather do, sir." He made a stride toward that goal in 2002 by directing his first film. (Poitier has done nine.) *Antwone Fisher,* the true story of a troubled sailor helped by a Navy psychiatrist (played by Washington), opened to warm reviews. Scripted by Fisher himself, the film, some believed, could earn Washington another Oscar. Not necessary, he said. "Winning for me is Antwone Fisher saying I did a good job."

J.K. Rowling

'WRITE, GOOD WOMAN, WRITE!' GOADED *POTTER* FANS. BUT THE AUTHOR WAS, WELL, MUM

SHE'S HAD TWO YEARS!" SAID EMMA SMITH, 12, A *Harry Potter* reader from Maryland. "I mean, when I have to do my homework I procrastinate, but I still get it done in time." To be sure, Potterites could hit the cineplex for a fix—the second film, *Chamber of Secrets,* premiered in November. But after cranking out four books in four years, Rowling, 37, was taking her time, noting that "I'm a perfectionist, and I want a bit more of a tweak." She was also distracted by a drawn-out plagiarism trial (decided in her favor). Then in September, Rowling (already mother of a daughter, 9) and her second husband, Neil Murray, 31, an anesthesiologist, announced that they expected a new potential Potter dependent in the spring.

Dr. Phil McGraw

OPRAH'S SIDEKICK PROVED HIMSELF A SOLO SUCCESS

LIFE IS A FULL-CONTACT SPORT. AND THERE'S A SCORE UP ON THE board." This and other nuggets of therapeutic Texas gold set Dr. Phil apart from the talk show competition. The Dallas-based psychologist and trial consultant (he had helped Winfrey defend herself against litigious beef bullies) gave up his guest spot on her show for his very own. With the invaluable Oprah seal of approval (and a commitment not to compete in the same time slots), his syndicated hour-long shrink sessions reached an unprecedented 97 percent of the U.S. market. McGraw, 52, a married father of two, commutes to L.A. for tapings. But don't expect him to conform to other California talk show rites. "I'm not doing makeovers, and I'm sure as hell not doing fashion shows," he said. "I have every intention of being faithful to that phrase, 'Make sure you dance with who brung ya.'"

Steve Fossett

A DAREDEVIL ADVENTURER FROM THE WINDY CITY BREEZED TO A NEW FIRST IN FLIGHT

COMPETE IN THE IDITAROD? CHECK. SWIM THE English Channel? Check. Circumnavigate the globe in a hot-air balloon? After six years of failed attempts (one almost fatal), the Chicago commodities broker finally crossed that last exploit off his adventure agenda, becoming the first to do it solo. Departing from Northam, Australia, on June 18 and cruising at up to 200 mph, he completed the spin in a mere 14 days. Accommodations weren't first-class in his closet-size cockpit—he had to breathe through an oxygen mask and use a bucket as his loo. After a rough landing, Fossett, 58, toasted his triumph with Bud Light (his sponsor). He also announced the end of his ballooning career, donating his *Spirit of Freedom* airship to the Smithsonian, where it now hangs next to Charles Lindbergh's historic *Spirit of St. Louis*.

Sarah Hughes

A U.S. TEEN TURNED AROUND A TARNISHED OLYMPICS

A HIGH SCHOOL JUNIOR AIMING FOR THE 1500S ON her SATs, Hughes pulled off a nifty bit of math at the Salt Lake City Olympics, becoming the first skater ever to leap from a seemingly doomed fourth after the short program to first overall. Trailing favorites Michelle Kwan, Russia's Irina Slutskaya and upstart Sasha Cohen, Hughes felt sure she would go home to Great Neck, New York, without a medal. That freed her to skate the long program of a lifetime—including two triple-triple combination jumps, a women's first. Her palpable joy of the sport lit up the skating competition, otherwise clouded by a Russian/French judging scandal (which resulted in two sets of gold medals in the pairs). Hughes, 16, did have her SAT prep book in Utah but amid the excitement put off the exam date.

Leonardo DiCaprio

WHERE'S LEO? M.I.A. FOR ALMOST TWO YEARS, HE RESURFACED AND ENDED THE YEAR WITH A BANG

HE'D GIVEN THEM NOTHING SINCE that *Beach* bummer back in 2000, and Leo fanatics were losing faith. (A readers' poll in *Seventeen* magazine even gave Christina Applegate better odds for a comeback.) Then in December the DiCaprio drought ended dramatically with a double dose of crime capers pitting Leo vs. Leo at the nation's box offices. Martin Scorsese's Irish Mob tale *Gangs of New York* featured Thug Leo opposite Cameron Diaz. Five days later, Steven Spielberg's *Catch Me If You Can* opened, starring Con Artist Leo pursued by Tom Hanks. No longer coupled with Brazilian supermodel Gisele Bündchen, the actor, 28, played the ever-available field and larked around with best bud Tobey Maguire, attending Lakers games or recording Beatles songs at London's hallowed Abbey Road Studios.

Ashanti

AFTER LENDING HER VOICE TO
OTHERS' HIT SINGLES, SHE
SET A RECORD OF HER OWN

AT 12, SINGING GOT HER busted by her mom. She was supposed to turn off the radio and do her chores. Why, then, could her mother still hear Mary J. Blige's voice rising upstairs? "I told her it wasn't the radio, it was me," recalled Ashanti Douglas. Her parents made a demo and helped Ashanti win a recording contract at age 14. Introduced to the world in 2002 as a guest vocalist on songs by Ja Rule and Fat Joe, Ashanti saw her debut CD enter *Billboard* at No. 1. When her own first single, "Foolish," hit the charts alongside the two she had appeared on earlier, she matched a record set by the Beatles: three singles in the Top 10. Raised in a New York City suburb, Ashanti was offered a track scholarship to Princeton (she set her high school's triple jump record). But she put college on hold to pursue music. Among those agreeing with that choice was the Soul Train awards panel, which gave her its Lady of Soul title despite an Internet petition by 30,000 objectors who felt she was too much of a neophyte. (The award honors the year's work, it was explained, not a whole career.) Also in her corner is collaborator Ja Rule. "Ashanti's voice is angelic," he said. "It's real soft but strong. That's a crazy thing to have." Yet the singer is grounded, despite her crazy success at 21. "Everyone's trying to convince me to move out," she said, referring to her parents' place. "But I love being at home."

Stephen King

HORRORS! THE MASTER OF THE PAGE-TURNER CLOSED THE BOOK ON HIS PUBLISHING CAREER

EVEN HE COULDN'T SAY HOW MUCH MONEY HE'S got—$100 million? Whatever. In King's estimation, it's enough. So after 50 books, the last of which was 2002's *From a Buick 8,* King, 55, told the world that it had seen its last possessed car, telekinetic teenager and rabid dog. Sort of. He will knock out three more installments in his *Dark Tower* series, which he began in college. And he's working on other projects, like a musical with John Mellencamp. (He does like to scare us, doesn't he?) He reminded disappointed fans that his oeuvre might have been over after he was struck by a van in 1999. (He calls life after the accident "the bonus round.") King did say that he would still write every day, just not publish. Perhaps he should take it easy. As we learned from *The Shining,* all work and no play makes Jack a dull boy.

The Miners of Black Wolf

WORD OF THEIR RESCUE AFTER 77 HOURS UNDERGROUND GAVE US ALL SOME MUCH-NEEDED GOOD NEWS

WE WERE JUST DOING WHAT WE DO every day—moving coal," said Ron Hileman, a 30-year mining veteran, of that July morning. But when drilling accidentally punctured a wall separating Pennsylvania's Black Wolf mine from an abandoned and flooded adjoining mine, he and eight others found themselves immersed in some 50 million gallons of swiftly rising water. "There was no way we were going to outrun it," said Hileman, 49 (third from right), a married father of two daughters. Wet, cold and in the dark, the nine men huddled together for warmth and emotional support. They shared a single corned beef sandwich and a few Life Savers and listened to the rescue team drilling 240 feet above to free them from what could have become their watery tomb. More than a day had passed when a lunch box floated by. They split its contents, then filled it with letters to their families—to be read in the event of their demise. "You can't imagine the thoughts in your head when death is right there," said Hileman. Perhaps the low point occurred when the sounds of drilling suddenly stopped. (A 1,500-pound drill bit had broken.) "We were thinking, did they take a coffee break or what?" he recalled. At 1 a.m. on the third day, rescuers found and pulled miner Randall Fogle, 43, to the surface. Within an hour all nine were out, having suffered only minor injuries. "It was like watching my children come into the world," said Pennsylvania Governor Mark Schweiker, who stayed at the scene throughout. His feelings were echoed across a nation grown weary of stories about terror threats and corporate greed. Always in the market for good news, the Disney corporation snapped up the rights to the men's stories for $150,000 each and retold them as a TV movie. That was fine with Hileman, who said of his job, "If my family has a say, I won't be going back."

Marissa Winokur

A NEW BROADWAY BABY STRUCK
A VICTORY FOR BIG BOUFFANTS AND
PLUS-SIZE GALS EVERYWHERE

IT LITERALLY TOOK ALL OF MY ENERGY not to burst out crying," said Winokur, 29, of *Hairspray*'s opening night. "It was the day I'd been waiting for my entire life." For years the actress had found steady work—in small film parts and in *Grease* on Broadway. But, as a 5-foot, size-12 woman, she never expected to be a headliner. "In the real world, size 12 is just normal," said the former high school cheerleader. "I always laugh and say, 'I'm showbiz fat.'" In *Hairspray* (based on the 1988 John Waters film about a teen's crusade to appear on and racially integrate a '60s TV dance show), Winokur helped create Broadway's biggest musical smash since *The Producers*. But the star is happiest playing to a particular audience: girls growing up with weight issues. "If I can make a difference by just being who I am," she said, "that means more than anything."

Tobey Maguire

A MOODY, CEREBRAL ACTOR PUMPED UP TO PLAY YOUR FRIENDLY NEIGHBORHOOD MOVIE SUPERHERO

SHOULD HE PICK UP ANY AWARDS FOR HIS ROLE IN *Spider-Man,* Maguire might thank his trainer. The thoughtful star of films based on novels like *The Ice Storm* and *Wonder Boys,* Maguire, 27, had proven acting chops. But could he open a summer flick based on a comic book? To convince the producers, he hit the gym like a man possessed. "I worked very hard to get that body," said Maguire, who wound up wowing fans as both the web-slinging superhero and his bookish alter ego. *Spider-Man*'s first weekend earned a record $114 million, and an unlikely action star was born. For pals like actress Sara Gilbert, it was no surprise. "He has a strong side, a very masculine side," she said. "It's just not the side that Hollywood saw first."

Shakira

WIELDING A GUITAR, A BIG VOICE
AND HIPS THAT WON'T QUIT, SHE
INTRODUCED AMERICANS TO
HER LATIN-ARABIC ROCK FUSION

A STAR IN HER NATIVE COLOMBIA since age 13, Shakira wanted to master English before recording her first album for an American audience. While it certainly helped that she learned to write in English—foreign tongues have a tough time on the U.S. pop charts—Shakira, 25, clinched her success here with her fluency in the international language of swiveling hips. The daughter of a Lebanese father and a Colombian mother, she has been belly dancing since childhood. When she set her hiphuggers ashake on MTV, it helped move 10 million copies of her 2001 crossover album *Laundry Service.* Then in 2002 she made a clean sweep of five categories at MTV's Latin Music Awards. Dating Antonio de la Rua, 28, the Buenos Aires-based lawyer son of a former Argentine president, Shakira launched a 30-nation concert itinerary she dubbed Tour of the Mongoose. Why? "It's an animal that looks like a rat, but you know what? It is an animal that can defeat the snake with just a bite. It's a living miracle, because if there is an animal on this earth that can defeat the snake with a bite, I think there's got to be some way for us to defeat or to bite the neck of hatred in this world, no?" *Si.*

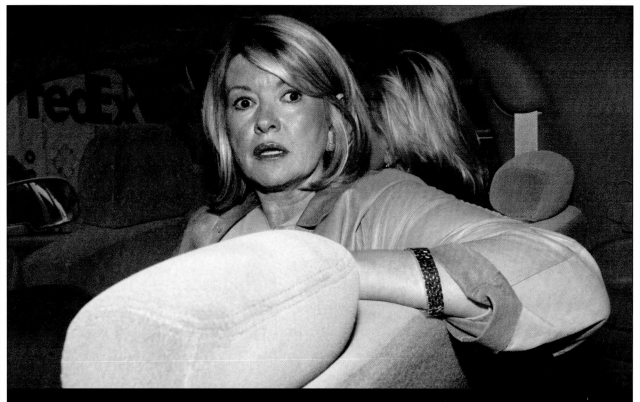

Martha Stewart

FOR THE CEO OF DOMESTIC DIVADOM, ACCUSATIONS OF INSIDER TRADING WERE NOT A GOOD THING

BUILT ON HER PERFECTIONIST PERSONALITY, STEWART'S billion-dollar empire took a heavy hit—her own net worth fell $100 million on paper in a day— as a result of an investigation into a relatively meager profit from the sale of ImClone stock in late 2001. Was the trade triggered by a heads-up from a family friend, ImClone founder Sam Waksal? Stewart, 61, had unloaded nearly 4,000 shares just before an announcement that the company's newest cancer drug failed to win FDA approval. It was an innocent, unrelated act, she said. Still, a congressional inquiry did little for her image, her company's most valued asset. Stewart suspended her weekly appearances on *The Early Show* and canceled her annual prime-time Christmas special. Shareholders sued over the mega-damage, leaving Stewart in a mess even she had no tips for tidying.

Patrick Tillman

MOVED BY 9/11, A FOOTBALLER MADE A SWITCH

THE WORD "HERO" DID OVERTIME IN 2001. THE FIRE- fighters at the World Trade Center and the Flight 93 passengers who faced down their hijackers—they were certainly heroes. A month later Barry Bonds was hailed as a hero for shattering baseball's home run record, though some carped that he wasn't exactly a team player. Then in 2002 a different sort of athlete redefined the term. In May, Tillman, a National Football League safety, walked away from a $3.6 million contract with the Arizona Cardinals to enlist in the U.S. Army. The California-born newlywed didn't publicize his career change. Instead, after promising to return to the NFL in three years, Tillman, 26, quietly headed to boot camp and an $18,000 salary to help defend his country. And to remind us what "hero" really means.

Sarah Jessica Parker

OFFSCREEN, TV'S MOST ADAMANT SINGLE GIRL DEMONSTRATED PREGNANCY WITH PANACHE: WEAR HEELS AND SEND YOUR HUSBAND OUT FOR SNACKS

S*EX AND THE CITY* COLUMNIST CARRIE BRADSHAW would have been proud of how alter ego Parker, 37, carried off her pregnancy. Even when her belly ballooned in the final weeks, the ever-fashionable actress was seen out and about teetering on her Manolo Blahniks. (Just days before delivering, she even showed up at a dinner honoring her favorite shoe designer.) But fans of the show, though supportive of Parker, were peeved that the season had to be cut short when her clingy costumes could no longer conceal the baby bump. With work on hold, Parker enjoyed the months leading up to motherhood. She sent husband Matthew Broderick, 40, and occasionally their pal Cady Huffman (his onstage love interest when he starred on Broadway in *The Producers*) out to hunt and gather Popeye's chicken or other cravings. Then her October 25 due date came and went. Still, she was out on the town. On the 28th, after dining at a French-Vietnamese restaurant not far from her Greenwich Village brownstone, Parker checked into Manhattan's Lenox Hill Hospital. Within hours the couple greeted a 6-pound, 8-ounce son, James Wilkie Broderick, named for Matthew's dad, the late star of TV's *Family*. Visitors to her bedside included gravid *Sex* costar Cynthia Nixon, who reported that shortly after giving birth Parker had already dropped much of her pregnancy weight. When the family emerged four days later, Parker and Broderick introduced a pashmina-wrapped James to 100 or so photographers and fans camped outside. There were the spindly high heels again. And two starstruck smiles. Said Broderick: "We're very happy."

Bernard Cardinal Law

AFTER YEARS OF PROTECTING
PRIESTS ACCUSED OF CHILD ABUSE,
A CHURCH LEADER FINALLY
RECOGNIZED A 'TERRIBLE EVIL'

I DID NOT, AS A MATTER OF POLICY, IN 1984, '85, '86, . . . '99, 2000, 2001, go to parishes on the occasion of dealing with a priest against whom an allegation of sexual abuse of a child had been made. I see now that that should have been done." So explained Boston's archbishop, Cardinal Law, 71, at a deposition in a suit filed by three victims of Father Paul Shanley. Law, they charged, had reassigned the priest though he had been accused of molesting children; Shanley had also endorsed "man-boy love" in a public meeting. After press reports about another Boston priest, Father John Geoghan—whose sexual abuse of some 150 children since 1966 led the church to agree to $10 million in secret settlements, with more pending—thousands of complaints about predatory priests came in from across the U.S.

The dialogue with the Catholic hierarchy was spearheaded by the Survivors Network of those Abused by Priests (SNAP); its director, David Clohessey, 45, had been a victim during his altar boy years. Voice of the Faithful—a rapidly growing national group seeking lay participation in church governance—joined in the outcry. In response, the United States Conference of Catholic Bishops retained an ex-FBI official to investigate; it also announced a "zero tolerance" policy but later modified it, after Vatican objections, to bring Rome into the judging process. Boston's Cardinal Law stonewalled at first but finally acknowledged the "terrible evil," asked "forgiveness of those who have been abused" and in mid-December resigned as archbishop.

Jimmy Fallon

SWEET-FACED, TALENTED AND FUNNY, HE WAS THE
LATE-NIGHT COMIC A GIRL COULD BRING HOME
TO MOM—AND PLENTY WISHED TO DO JUST THAT

IT SOUNDS EXACTLY LIKE THE SORT OF POP-CULTURE
flotsam that Fallon himself would spoof on *Saturday
Night Live.* But how do you handle a Web site called
"The Jimmy Fallon Love Shrine," in which your online
fans describe you as "the superfox of the century?"
SNL, where Fallon mans the Weekend Update desk
with Tina Fey, has given the world some great comedy
stars, but rarely does it spin out a heartthrob. "His
funniness just adds to his cuteness," cooed Kirsten Dunst,
with whom Fallon, 28, hosted the MTV Movie Awards
in 2001. A year later he returned as solo emcee of the
MTV Video Music Awards, an appropriate assignment
for a comic whose act relies heavily on send-ups of pop
stars (Coldplay, Dave Matthews and U2 were recent tar-
gets). He also captured his fusion of music and comedy
in the album *The Bathroom Wall.* (Devoid of bathroom
humor or anything R-rated, the release didn't carry a
"parental warning" label, to Fallon's feigned chagrin.)
Though he professed no immediate plans to graduate
from *SNL,* Fallon is dabbling in acting, having shot
HBO's *Band of Brothers* and Woody Allen's upcoming
Anything Else. For the moment he is enjoying his current level of fame, refreshingly cognizant of the fact
that it someday will be a memory. "When I'm 60 I'm
going to be begging people to recognize me," he said.
"I'll be walking around with a T-shirt that says, 'Hey,
I was on Weekend Update.'"

Michael Jackson

NO LONGER INVINCIBLE ON THE CHARTS, THE KING OF POP SAW HIS SIDESHOW LIFE TAKE CENTER STAGE

SONY CHIEF TOMMY MOTTOLA HAS CHAMPIONED the careers of many African-Americans. So why did Jackson brandish a homemade sign outside his New York City office and call him "a racist"? Industry insiders posited it was a reaction to declining record sales and fortunes (as he faced lawsuits and perhaps $200 million in debts). Or maybe it was the stresses of a growing family: He had recently fathered a third child—his second named Prince. (The mother remained a mystery.) But on his 44th birthday he could put career woes aside when Britney Spears presented him with the "artist of the millennium" honor at the MTV Video Music Awards. Jackson was moved, only to learn later that there was no such title. Spears, in her birthday wishes, had in her view simply believed that he was the artist of the millennium.

Charlton Heston

THE ACTOR AND LOBBYIST FACED A NEW FIGHT

I WANTED TO PREPARE A FEW WORDS FOR YOU NOW, because when the time comes, I may not be able to," declared Heston, 78, in a videotape released to share the sad news that he was suffering from early signs of Alzheimer's disease. Serious but in good spirits, he continued, "If I tell you a funny story for the second time, laugh anyway." The Oscar winner, who appeared in the 2002 documentary *Bowling for Columbine* in his capacity as National Rifle Association president, said he hoped to continue acting and would serve out a final term at the NRA. Well-wishers included Nancy Reagan, whose husband, the former President, suffers from Alzheimer's, and Sarah Brady, an antigun advocate and wife of James Brady, who was shot during the 1981 attempt on Reagan's life.

Serena Williams

WITH ONE, TWO, THREE GRAND SLAM WINS OVER VENUS, SHE MATCHED BIG SISTER'S TOTAL AND ASSUMED HER NO. 1 SEED

ROWING UP IN CALIFORNIA, ALL SERENA WILLIAMS WANTED TO BE WAS Venus Williams. "When we would go out to eat, my parents made me order first, or else I would order everything Venus ordered," she admitted. Now Venus may want what Serena's got. A month after beating big sis at the French Open, Serena, 21, dethroned Venus, 22, from tennis's top spot and proceeded to whip her at Wimbledon. And then one more time at the U.S. Open. Now each has won four Grand Slams. The on-court rivalry aside, the Williamses remain tight, helping each other through their parents' divorce, finalized in October. And at restaurants. "I still have to know what Venus is getting," she told *Ebony*. "But now we'll get different things, so we can share."

Chelsea Clinton

WHO'S THAT GIRL? MADONNA'S NEWEST PAL IS
A FUN-LOVING, GLOBE-TROTTING GRAD STUDENT
WHO ADORES COUTURE AND HER NEW GUY

THE FORMER FIRST DAUGHTER INHERITED A LOT FROM her parents: the smarts to get into Oxford, poise under pressure—and a head of persistently curly hair. So when Clinton, 22, appeared in the front row of a Versace show in Paris with a new stick-straight bob, she did more than make a fashion statement—she put a little distance between her and her familial roots (at least until the next shampoo). All grown up in spike heels and smoky eye shadow, Clinton seemed at last to have been asked to sit at the cool kids' table, taking in the Versace collection seated next to Madonna and Gwyneth Paltrow (who sported similarly glossy dos). Having passed four years at Stanford as a studiously normal undergrad, Clinton had begun taking advantage of her celebrity birthright as an international-relations postgrad at Oxford. She turned up in clubs, at movie premieres and at hip London eateries. She cavorted with movie and rock stars including Kevin Spacey, Bono and Paul McCartney. The English press (which gave her a wrist slap in 2001, after she wrote in a U.S. magazine that she felt anti-American sentiment in Europe after 9/11) came to embrace her. The society mag *Tatler* named her the fifth most eligible woman in England. But sorry, lads, as Clinton herself announced—oh, yes, she talks to the media now—she's completely in love with her schoolmate Ian Klaus, 24, a Californian who, like her dad, is a Rhodes Scholar. The newly polished exchange student also set the record straight on her high-profile gallivanting. "I don't do as much partying as people think I do," she said. "My main priority is studying. And being with Ian."

Bernie Mac

A GRUFF-LOVE SITCOM HIT
MADE AMERICA CRY UNCLE

WHEN BILL MURRAY BOWED out as Bosley, who would replace him in *Charlie's Angels 2*? Good morning, Bernie. "We're brothers from a different mother," cracked Mac of his casting for the 2003 sequel. Of course, the 45-year-old stand-up comic is a master of complex family dynamics. In TV's *Bernie Mac Show* he plays a brash but lovable uncle raising his pugnacious nephew and nieces. And in his own life, Mac and his wife have a daughter, 25, and took in his teenage niece and her daughter. The Chicago-born Mac drove a Wonder Bread truck before touring with the Original Kings of Comedy. After a rejection by ABC, Fox finally green-lighted the series that emerged as one of the biggest crossover black sitcom hits since *Cosby,* got Mac an Emmy nod and won the far more prestigious Peabody Award.

Jimmy Carter

ROSALYNN CARTER THOUGHT THE 4 A.M. CALL WAS a joke. No, it really was Oslo phoning to say that her oft-nominated husband, 78, had finally won the Nobel Prize. The Georgian had been recognized for his role in the 1978 Camp David accords plus his post-presidential work "waging peace" from Bosnia to Sudan and monitoring elections in nascent democracies.

But the award, noted Nobel chair Gunnar Berge, also "should be interpreted as a criticism" of President Bush's approach to Iraq. (Carter has said he opposes unilateral action but would not condemn Bush, who congratulated him.) Weighing the honor against Carter's reelection defeat in 1980, historian Douglas Brinkley declared, "He has wiped the word 'loser' off his chest."

Alice Sebold

A DARK FICTION DEBUT SIGNALED A WRITER'S BRIGHT FUTURE

THE 14-YEAR-OLD NARRATOR IS DEAD ON PAGE ONE. A GRIM, literary first novel about a rape and murder, it wasn't going to be a beach read. But in October *The Lovely Bones* perched on the bestseller list atop names like Stephen King and Tom Clancy. Sebold, 39, was thinking "maybe five people would read her book," said her husband, writer Glen David Gold (*Carter Beats the Devil*), 38. Instead she sold more than a million. In a summer when too many headlines told of too many abducted girls, Sebold inadvertently but artfully tapped into a tender part of the nation's psyche. "People are finding it a healing book," observed Sebold, a Philadelphian whose earlier work was a memoir about surviving her own rape in 1981. "One man said he felt it was a permission slip for grief."

Eminem

GIFTED ARTIST OR MENACE TO AMERICA'S YOUTH? THAT DEBATE GAVE WAY TO A NEW QUESTION: CAN HE ACT?

THE FILM *8 MILE,* WHICH TELLS A STORY OF an aspiring white rapper from Detroit, marked the screen debut of Marshall "Eminem" Mathers III, once an aspiring white rapper from Detroit. Though insisting it isn't strictly biographical, Mathers, 30, did allow that he drew on his own experience: "It's weird when you think I only had to go back about four years to find that point in my life." In that brief time he became, depending on your view, either a profound pied piper with a mike or a voice of angry young men leading followers into his vision of hell, where he fantasizes about killing his mother and (now ex-) wife, Kim (with whom he's reportedly reconciled). But art isn't life, Mathers maintained. If he were that angry, violent misogynist, he wouldn't be able to lovingly raise his daughter Hailie, 7. And when *8 Mile* was released, most reviewers agreed that Mathers was acting onscreen, not just being. A star is born.

Al Roker

POST-OP, *TODAY*'S GOURMAND BECAME TWO-THIRDS THE WEATHERMAN HE USED TO BE

LOOK AT THAT! AL'S GOT NO BUTT!" SQUEALED *TODAY* cohost Matt Lauer. At his original 320 pounds, there were no buts about it—Roker's rotund measurements warranted drastic measures. So in March, Roker, 48, underwent gastric bypass surgery. (Embarrassed, he told colleagues at the time that his gallbladder had to be removed.) Within eight months, the 5'8" meteorologist known to ingest Quarter Pounders in pairs caused double takes with his streamlined 220-pound frame. Now *20/20* correspondent Deborah Roberts, 42, can feel her husband's ribs when they hug, while Leila, 4, enjoys frequent piggyback rides. Infant Nicholas also gets more attention now that Roker can carry him upstairs with less huffing and puffing. "I'm down from four chins to two," said Roker, reveling in his smaller size and the big changes that resulted. "I'm never going back."

Jennifer Lopez & Ben Affleck

BEN LOVES JEN. JEN LOVES BEN (AND WEDDINGS).
SO JEWELERS AND PAPARAZZI LOVE BEN AND JEN

HE FILM CAREER. THE PERFUME NAMED FOR HER. The penchant for luxe jewels. And now the multiple marriages. Jennifer Lopez continued 2002 on a pace to become the Elizabeth Taylor of her generation. Shortly after her first wedding anniversary with second husband Cris Judd came up on the calendar, the singer-actress was engaged to be married to Ben Affleck, her costar in the films *Gigli* and *Jersey Girl*. The two stars met in the winter of 2001 on the set of *Gigli*. When filming wrapped, Affleck took an ad in *The Hollywood Reporter,* praising Lopez's "astonishing talent, real poise, and true grace." Disputing rumors to the contrary, they insisted that they didn't become a couple until Sunday, July 21, a few days after Lopez and Judd agreed to end their 10-month marriage (see page 78).

It seemed an eventful year for Affleck as well. He had kicked his problem with alcohol after a 2001 rehab stint, and in May he replaced Harrison Ford as Jack Ryan in Tom Clancy's *The Sum of All Fears*. Romantically he has proved himself a latter-day Richard Burton by showering Lopez with jewels—a yellow- and white-diamond bracelet the day before she filed for divorce, and then in the fall a custom-made, 6.1-carat pink Harry Winston diamond ring. Even before formally announcing the engagement, she showed off the gem in her video "Jenny from the Block," which dramatized the couple's paparazzi-dogged romance; Affleck played himself. Why the rush? She was newly 33, and on turning 30 in August, Affleck noted, "That's the point after which if you're not starting to think of marriage and having kids, you're immature and have a Peter Pan complex. I want to take those steps. I finally feel ready to do that." As for J.Lo, "when she wants to do something, she doesn't wait," said photographer pal Gilles Bensimon. "She wants it now." Alas, while you can hurry love, you can't hurry marriage. California law requires six months to finalize a divorce. So the soonest Ben and Jen could become husband and wife is January 27, 2003.

Salma Hayek

AS PRODUCER AND STAR OF *FRIDA,* SHE PAINTED A
MIGHTY NEW IMAGE OF HERSELF ON AN EPIC CANVAS

A HOMELY, CRIPPLED, COMMUNIST ARTIST WITH AN UNKEMPT unibrow—it was the role that screen siren Hayek dreamed of and doggedly pursued for eight years. The life of the late Mexican surrealist Frida Kahlo captivated fellow countrywoman Hayek, who had to contend with Madonna and Jennifer Lopez for rights to the story. Taking on the job of producer as well, Hayek toiled to put together *Frida*'s $12 million budget and to handpick a powerful cast, including Ashley Judd, Geoffrey Rush, Alfred Molina and her boyfriend Edward Norton, 33, who helped rewrite the script at no charge. The daughter of an opera diva and a hardware store owner, Hayek, 36, starred in Mexico's leading soap before moving north in 1991. Typecast as the curvaceous sexpot with an accent in action films like *Desperado,* she was underestimated—pre-*Frida.* "People think that she is some hot tamale," said costar Molina. "Let me put it this way: If she was white and male, she'd be Harvey Weinstein by now."

Paul Burrell

CLEARED OF THEFT CHARGES, PRINCESS DI'S FORMER BUTLER SOLD SCANDALOUS SECRETS TO THE PRESS

THE PRINCESS WENT OUT TO MEET A LOVER WEARING nothing but a fur coat. Prince Philip wrote letters to Diana calling her a "trollop" and a "harlot." Prince Charles made his valet hold the jar while he gave a urine specimen. On trial for allegedly stealing some 310 items from Diana's estate (including the signet ring of her lover James Hewitt), the butler who once insisted such secrets were "safe with me" spilled 39 pages of such unsavory details of palace life in his deposition. A day before he was to repeat them in open court, Burrell got a dramatic reprieve when the Queen suddenly remembered that he had told her in 1997 that he was storing some of Diana's valuables. His trial was over. But once the deposition was unsealed, so were the butler's lips. Hassled and humiliated by almost two years of investigations, Burrell, 44, struck a $470,000 deal with the *Daily Mirror* to tell all, including con-

firming that Diana had taped a conversation in which George Smith, then Prince Charles's valet, accused a palace aide of raping him. By then Smith was also blabbing to the tabs about a similar incident between another servant and a member of the royal family. Burrell, meanwhile, signed on to host a game show called *What the Butler Saw* and then flew to New York City for a publicity tour with his wife and two sons.

Feeling the pressure, Charles ordered an unprecedented internal investigation. And ironically, in November, on his 54th birthday, the heir to the throne got what should have been happy news—the Church of England had lifted the ban on the remarriage of divorcés. Had the Church been so permissive back in the 1980s, when he was forced to choose Diana Spencer over longtime love Camilla Parker Bowles, so much dirty linen—not to mention human tragedy—might have been avoided.

Britney Spears

NEWLY UNATTACHED, POP'S PRINCESS TOOK A
SELF-IMPOSED SABBATICAL. OR TRIED TO, ANYWAY

F OR BRITNEY, WHO'S USED TO RUNNING AT 90 MILES PER
hour, it's hard to slow down," observed the star's
mom, Lynne. Spears, 21, announced she would
be taking a six-month break from her celebrity duties as
soon as her tour ended on July 28. (The final show, in
Mexico City, wound up sourly, as rain caused Spears to
cut the concert short after five songs. She fled the arena
to resounding boos and later took flak for making a
rude hand gesture to the Mexican paparazzi.) "I give it
a couple of months," said Lynne, 47, of her daughter's
plan to unwind. Momma knew best. Earlier in the
summer Spears's Manhattan restaurant Nyla opened, and
she committed herself to showing up enough to promote it. In August she was a presenter at both the MTV
Video Music Awards and the Teen Choice Awards. In
September she did find enough time off to lounge about
her new Hollywood Hills mansion, venturing out to
ogle the home of Brad Pitt and Jennifer Aniston. "I
stood on top of my car, trying to see in," she admitted.
"I honestly don't know what to do with myself." So
back to work it was in October, when she jetted to
Milan to take part in new pal Donatella Versace's fashion
show. By November she was in England, recording her
next album. So much for the break. And the breakup.
Spotted on a London street wearing a T-shirt that read
"Dump Him," Spears was decidedly unsentimental
about her March split from Justin Timberlake, 21. (See
page 61.) "This may sound weird," she said, "but I'm the
happiest I've been in a long freakin' time."

Coleen Rowley

AN FBI AGENT BLEW THE WHISTLE TO REVEAL RED TAPE THAT MAY HAVE PROVEN DEADLY ON 9/11

COULD THE AL-QAEDA ATTACKS HAVE BEEN THWART-ed? It's almost too painful a hypothetical to consider. But it was a possibility raised in a 13-page letter sent by FBI agent Rowley, 47, to the agency's director, Robert Mueller, and several members of Congress. The statement charged headquarters with hampering attempts by Rowley's Minnesota office to investigate flight student Zacarias Moussaoui, later on trial as the "20th hijacker." Her conclusion: "It's at least pos-sible we could have gotten lucky and uncovered one or two more of the terrorists in flight training prior to September 11." Rowley, whose husband stays home with their four kids, put her job on the line by writing the letter—one angry ex-agent compared her to convicted traitor Robert Hanssen. But the no-nonsense lawyer (she wore a fanny pack to a Senate appearance, above) had the backing of her boss in Minneapolis. "As long as she wants to stay," she said, "she stays."

The Alvarez Sisters

ONCE JOINED AT THE HEAD, TWINS BEAT THE ODDS

BORN BY C-SECTION IN A RURAL GUATEMALAN CLINIC after their mother, Alba Leticia Alvarez, 22, labored for eight days, Maria Teresa and Maria de Jesus entered the world joined at the top of their heads. "I was shocked," said dad Wenceslao Quiej Lopez, 21, a banana packer. "But I had to accept it. They were my daughters." Hospitalized for a year in Guatemala City, Maria de Jesus was the shier girl, while Maria Teresa, nurses found, was more boisterous. "We have to do something so they can be two independent human beings," vowed neurosurgeon Jorge Lazareff of UCLA's Mattel Children's Hospital, which covered most of the $1.5 million in costs. In 22 hours Lazareff's team of 50 separated the girls. Miraculously, both survived and were due to return home, where, said one volunteer on the case, "they had become national treasures."

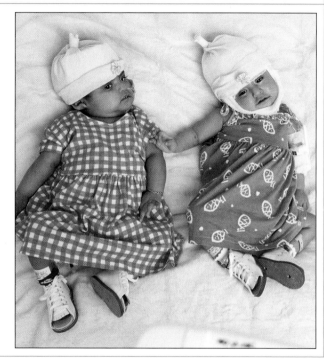

Nia Vardalos

FICTIONALIZING HER BIG, FUNNY FAMILY TREE, SHE CREATED A RUNAWAY HIT

PENNING AND PERFORMING YOUR OWN one-woman show is a great way to break into the biz. Getting Tom Hanks to see it is even better. He and wife Rita Wilson (whose family is Greek) thought Vardalos's *My Big Fat Greek Wedding* would make a terrific little flick. Costing just $5 million, it wound up being the most profitable indie film ever and one of the Top 100 grossers of all time. Capping her big year, Vardalos, 40, dined in her native Winnipeg with Queen Elizabeth. Her Majesty noted that Prince Philip is Greek and that they planned to see the film. "I got this image of the two of them buying popcorn," said Vardalos, who is married to *The Drew Carey Show*'s Ian Gomez, 38, "and her having to take off her tiara so the people behind her could see."

Sylvia Ann Hewlett

HER CONTROVERSIAL BOOK ASSERTED THAT HIGH-POWERED CAREER WOMEN CAN'T TRUMP BIOLOGY

O F THE 42 PERCENT OF FEMALE EXECS WHO ARE childless past 40, a mere 14 percent say they skipped having kids by choice. That statistic, argued economist Hewlett in her book *Creating a Life,* reveals that U.S. women are deluding themselves that they can have it all late in life; part of the problem, she added, is the "hype" about assisted reproduction success rates. Hewlett, 56, who bore her fourth child (Emma, above) at 51, raised feminist ire by instructing women to be "intentional" about procreating early. *SNL*'s Tina Fey, 32, spoke for many, countering, "Sylvia's right. I definitely should have had a baby when I was 27, living in Chicago over a biker bar, pulling down a cool $12,000 a year. That would have worked out great."

Rep. Nancy Pelosi

IN A FIRST, SHE BECAME THE DEMS' HEAD OF HOUSE

S HE WAITED UNTIL THE LAST OF HER FIVE KIDS WAS IN college to run for office—and for Congress yet. But Pelosi knew the ropes: Her dad, Tommy D'Alesandro Jr., had been a scrappy Baltimore congressman and mayor. Pelosi (who had moved to San Francisco) won, and 16 years later, at 62, will take over the House Democrats. The first woman ever to become party leader in either chamber, she quipped, "I've been waiting 200 years for this." Pelosi votes liberal, including a "nay" on President Bush's war proposal. But that doesn't necessarily preclude their working together. It was her daughter Alexandra, 32, a leftish TV journalist, who charmed Bush into cooperating on her lighthearted documentary *Journeys with George,* which aired election night on HBO.

Justin Timberlake

AFTER BIDDING BRITNEY 'BYE BYE BYE,' THE
'N SYNCER ALSO WENT IT ALONE ON A NEW CD

"THERE ARE NIGHTS WHEN YOU CRY YOURSELF TO sleep," admitted Timberlake, 21, after ending a four-year relationship with former *Mickey Mouse Club* castmate Britney Spears, rendering himself all the more puppylike to his smitten fans. But heartbreak provided inspiration. He avoided a straight answer about what caused the split but expressed himself in a well-received first solo album, *Justified,* which was full of lovesick lyrics like "You don't have to say what you did/ I already know." (He swore the project didn't mean the end of his band, but what else was he supposed to do while Lance Bass was—fruitlessly as it turned out—training at Russian space camp?) While he was also vague in his denials about seeing *Charmed* star Alyssa Milano, 29, and Janet Jackson, 36, he did forthrightly address one false rumor that had him and Britney doing battle in a nightclub dance-off. Declared Timberlake, laughing: "I would kill her in a dance-off."

Christopher Reeve

BY REGAINING LIMITED MOVEMENT, THE ACTOR-
TURNED-ACTIVIST AMAZED SCIENTISTS AND
INSPIRED MILLIONS WITH SPINAL-CORD INJURIES

N A SEPTEMBER 2000 CHAT WITH HIS WIFE, DANA, CHRIS-
topher Reeve underscored a point by raising the index
finger of his left hand. Made by anyone else, the same
gesture would have gone unnoticed. But Dana, who
had seen her husband sit achingly still in a wheelchair
since an equestrian accident in 1995, caught it immedi-
ately. "Did you do that on purpose?" she asked. He
hadn't. "Well, try," she urged him. He found that he
could make his finger obey the command of his brain,
something that should be impossible for a person like
Reeve, with damage to his spinal cord at the second
cervical vertebra in his neck. After showing the renewed
movement to his doctor, Reeve began an intensified reg-
imen of exercise, which may have helped rejuvenate
more of his nervous system's circuitry. While some
experts cautioned that Reeve's development is unlikely
to be duplicated in most spinal-cord patients, others
heralded it as indicative of a possible breakthrough.

This year Reeve, 50, continued to make progress with
his unorthodox therapy and kept lobbying for stem cell
research funding, believing that it remains the best hope
for a cure. By September, when he published a book,
Nothing Is Impossible: Reflections on a New Life, the
Superman star could wiggle fingers and toes, flex one
wrist, and take a few assisted steps in a swimming pool.
He could breathe without a respirator for nearly two
hours. Moreover, he had regained some sense of touch.
Now he could feel a hug from Dana, 41, or their son Will,
10. (He also has two grown children from a previous relationship, Alexandra and Matthew, a recent college grad
who filmed a documentary about his dad's daily life.)
"Dana likes to rest her hand on mine when we talk," said
Reeve. "Now I don't have to look to see that it's there."

THE CHAPEL

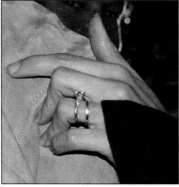

THE RINGS

THE NEWLYWEDS

Milestones

In 2002 marriage vets (Lisa Marie, Liza) and rookies (Gwen, Sarah Michelle) flocked to the altar and a few settled couples (Uma & Ethan, Johnny & Vanessa) expanded their broods. Alas, some of last year's brides (J.Lo, Drew) didn't make it to their first anniversary

JULY 4, 2002

Julia Roberts & Danny Moder

THEY COULD HAVE WED "AT A CASTLE OR THE FANCIEST HOTEL," SAID A FRIEND. "But that isn't her." Instead, the actress and the cameraman, who met on 2000's *The Mexican,* chose her Taos, New Mexico, ranch and billed the event as just an Independence Day barbecue. Roberts—who prepped with a facial and by weeding her garden—treated unaware guests to homemade turkey and pancakes. No one (except her sister, lawyer and dressmaker) expected wedding cake for dessert. Just the year before, she had split from Benjamin Bratt; Moder's divorce from makeup artist Vera Steimberg wasn't finalized until May. But come midnight, when many were thinking of turning in, Moder, 33, dropped to one knee and, before some 60 family members and friends—with hardly a celebrity in the bunch—asked Roberts, 34, to marry him. "Yes! Yes! Yes!" cried the Oscar winner, clutching her heart. "Yes! Yes! Yes!" cheered the crowd. Rejuvenated by the 20-minute, kiss-filled ceremony, the revelers celebrated till dawn. Exulted one attendee: "That girl can really throw a party."

SEPTEMBER 14, 2002, AND SEPTEMBER 26, 2002

Gwen Stefani & Gavin Rossdale

AFTER SIX YEARS OF DATING, THE SINGERS FOR NO DOUBT (STEFANI, 32) and Bush (Rossdale, 34) tied a double knot. They wed first in England (his homeland) and then in California (hers), with a church ceremony followed by a blowout at a pal's L.A. mansion. Guests in the U.S. included Brad Pitt, Jennifer Aniston and Ben Stiller. In London, both bands and the groom's Hungarian sheepdog were on hand. Said John Galliano, who made the pink-and-white silk gown worn on both continents: "She cried, he cried—and so did the dog."

JUNE 11, 2002

Heather Mills & Sir Paul McCartney

LISTEN, DO YOU WANT TO KNOW a secret? Do you promise not to tell?" Sir Jack Leslie, the octogenarian owner of the Irish estate that was the site of the McCartney-Mills wedding, either needed a brushup on his Beatles' lyrics or a refresher course in discretion. Days before the event, Sir Jack told reporters, "It's next Tuesday, but it's top secret." Thus tipped off, the press queued at the estate's 17th-century Protestant church to record the arrival of the groom's four kids (the eldest of whom is four years senior to the 34-year-old bride) plus rock royals Ringo Starr, Chrissie Hynde and Eric Clapton, among 300 other guests. Carrying 11 McCartney roses (named for Sir Paul in 1993), Mills walked the aisle in a dress of her own design to the strains of a march variation of "Heather" written by her 59-year-old mate. The reported $3.2 million affair included a vegetarian Indian banquet served on gold-leaf plates and a fireworks display. But, as with love, money couldn't buy the two rainbows that serendipitously arched across the sky just after the couple exited the church.

Sarah Michelle Gellar & Freddie Prinze Jr.

WAS IT THE LOVE OR THE HUmidity? "They glowed as they gazed at one another," reported one of the guests at the Costa Careyes, Mexico, union of generation Y's own Pickford and Fairbanks. Gellar, 25, and Prinze, 26, saw to every detail, from the Vera Wang bridesmaids' dresses to the salsa band to having pal Adam Shankman (director of *The Wedding Planner*) ordained over the Internet so he could officiate. But the *Scooby-Doo* costars couldn't have guessed that Hurricane Hernan would crash the party and force it indoors. Or that on their first full day of wedded bliss the resort where they had treated their guests to a four-day vacation would be rocked by a 4.6 earthquake. "Earthquake? Hurricane? All those bigger-than-life natural events can only bode well for the marriage," suggested Prinze family friend Ron DiBlasio. Cathy Waterman, who designed the couple's platinum rings, agreed, saying, "This is going to last."

AUGUST 10, 2002

Lisa Marie Presley & Nicolas Cage

THE LAVA FIELDS OF HAWAII'S BIG ISLAND SEEMED AN INAUSPICIOUS backdrop for the surprise nuptials of Elvis's only child and his devout actor fan, given their tempestuous romantic histories. The witnesses, hoping against hope, included the bride's mom, Priscilla, and the couple's three kids from prior relationships. But less than four months later, Cage, 38, filed for divorce, citing the accustomed irreconcilable differences. "I'm sad about this," said Presley, 34, whose most recent husband had been Michael Jackson. "But we shouldn't have been married in the first place. It was a big mistake."

MAY 31, 2002

Sharon Lawrence & Tom Apostle

THE DOCTOR, 39, DIDN'T RECOG-nize the former *NYPD Blue* star when they met in a hospital where he was treating a friend of hers. "I was attracted to his kindness," said Lawrence, 40. "We've had a delightful romance ever since." Apostle, a physiatrist, was not a regular viewer of the show and likely also didn't recognize the special significance of the church where the couple married after almost two years of dating: L.A.'s historic St. Sophia Greek Orthodox Cathedral was the site of the wedding between Lawrence's character and Dennis Franz's Andy Sipowicz.

JUNE 15, 2002

Denise Richards & Charlie Sheen

'M SURE DIFFERENT PEOPLE'S PERCEPTIONS ARE LIKE, 'OH, HOLLY-wood marriage, they just met; they'll be divorced in four months.' But we take it very seriously," said *Undercover Brother* star Richards, 31, who, with Sheen, 36, attended pre-wedding classes taught by a priest. True, they were engaged 12 weeks after they began dating, but there was no doubt in the minds of their 85 guests about the love between them. After the I dos, they "just kept kissing," said Sheen's *Spin City* pal Heather Locklear, who attended with husband Richie Sambora. Once a tabloid regular for his escapades with call girls and drugs, Sheen felt a bachelor party "would be redundant" and skipped that tradition. Said proud papa Martin of his son: "This is a rebirth of who he really is."

APRIL 13, 2002

Talisa Soto & Benjamin Bratt

IT'S LIKE BEING IN LOVE FOR THE FIRST time," said Bratt, apparently having wiped clean the memory of his last girlfriend, Julia Roberts. Less than a year after their breakup, the actor, 38, was betrothed to his *Piñero* costar, 35. In his brief return to singlehood, he had announced that with his next relationship, "my intention is to make her the mother of my children." Soto, too, had looked forward to parenthood, a fact that may have contributed to the end of her three-year marriage to actor Costas Mandylor. "She was gearing up for children, and it never happened," said a friend. Eagerness to start a family may explain the haste of the nuptials. The bride, they later revealed, was a few weeks pregnant.

JUNE 18, 2002

Morleigh Steinberg & The Edge

DESPITE THE CONVERGENCE of rock stars, actors and supermodels, this was "much more of a family wedding than a showbiz do," said one guest. After 10 years of dating and two children (Sian, 4, and Levi, 2), the U2 guitarist born David Evans, 40, made it official in a civil ceremony in Dublin with choreographer Steinberg, 37. Four days later they partied in a public garden amid the ruins of a medieval castle in Eze, France. Bono and the rest of U2—not to mention Dennis Hopper, Lenny Kravitz and models Christy Turlington and Helena Christensen—did make for a glittering guest list. But family fun prevailed when attendees competed in an egg-and-spoon race. Explained producer Howie B: "You place a spoon in your hand, an egg on top and run like a mother."

APRIL 20, 2002

Desiree Gruber & Kyle MacLachlan

IN THE END, IT ISN'T THE CONCH chowder or the eight-piece Latin band or the hand-sewn crystals on the bridal gown that you remember about a wedding. It's the unscripted little moments. You know, like when the best man loses the rings. "He was looking in his pocket and realized he had a hole in his lining," said Gruber, 34, of MacLachlan's brother Craig. "We were all laughing. I didn't mind at all." The rings were located, and Gruber, a publicist, was soon hitched to the *Sex and the City* actor, 43, who called their Miami nuptials, mishap and all, "magical."

AUGUST 25, 2002

Yasmine Bleeth & Paul Cerrito Jr.

THEIR MEETING WASN'T EXACTLY cute. In 2000 the former *Baywatch* babe checked into a Malibu rehab clinic and checked out with a new suitor. Together, Bleeth, 34, and Cerrito, 32, a Michigan nightclub owner, began building a new sober life. (Brief relapses landed him in jail and her on probation for cocaine possession.) Undaunted, they wed in a Santa Barbara, California, ceremony punctuated by smiles and tears that began with an unusual processional: Chris Isaak's "Wicked Game," in which the singer croons, "No I don't wanna fall in love with you."

FEBRUARY 17, 2002

Joan Collins & Percy Gibson

I'VE NEVER HAD A BIG WEDDING BE-fore," explained the actress about how these nuptials differed from her previous four. "They've always been on the rush in Vegas or Jamaica." Between 1951 and 1985, Collins ventured one marriage per decade, and despite the passage of time, all her mates had something in common: "Joan," said friend Connie Jones, "has never dated anyone over 40." At 68, the former *Dynasty* star kept her streak intact, marrying theater manager Gibson, 36, before 170 guests at Claridge's in London. "Weddings are always the hope against the experience," observed Collins's author pal Adrian Gill. "You write a blank check for the future. In Joan's case it is a very brave, very hopeful check to write."

FEBRUARY 23, 2002

LeAnn Rimes & Dean Sheremet

I CRIED THE WHOLE TIME," REPORTED RIMES'S FATHER, Wilbur, whom the singer had invited to the wedding only 10 days earlier. The two had recently settled a lawsuit in which she had charged him with fleecing her out of $7 million while comanaging her career. Rimes, 19, met Sheremet, 21, a dancer who appeared with her at a country music awards show, in 2001. Engaged a half year later, they wed in a chapel at Southern Methodist University in Dallas. The couple were "ecstatic," observed a Rimes friend. So were family members when LeAnn and Wilbur shared a moving father-daughter dance.

JUNE 8, 2002
Natalie Anne Bryant & Taylor Hanson

EVER SINCE *THE ED SULLIVAN SHOW* ran a title with John Lennon's face that read "Sorry girls, he's married," teen idols have known the value of appearing at least theoretically available to hopeful fans. But Hanson, 19, the most adored of the three singing brothers (Isaac and Zac are 21 and 16), was willing to cash in that currency for love. So when most guys his age are asking girls to the prom (the homeschooled son of evangelical Christians, Taylor didn't have a prom), the singer was proposing to his 18-year-old girlfriend. Soon rumors about a small Pine Mountain, Georgia, ceremony burned up the Internet. Hanson confirmed the news on the band's official Web site, writing, "Our wedding was exactly how we envisioned it. Natalie and I are looking forward to our life together."

JANUARY 12, 2002
Liza Powel & Conan O'Brien

FITTINGLY, THE TALK SHOW HOST'S MARRIAGE began with an opening monologue. His Harvard classmate, Rev. Paul O'Brien (no relation), did a few minutes about coffee in Seattle (the bride's hometown), then passed out cups in the pews of the city's St. James Cathedral. Powel, 31, an advertising executive, O'Brien, 38, and their 200 or so guests (including former *Late Night* sidekick Andy Richter) then moved to Union Station for a reception, where the groom grabbed a guitar and serenaded along with the Max Weinberg 7. Observed one guest fondly: "He probably shouldn't give up his night job."

MARCH 16, 2002

Liza Minnelli & David Gest

WHEN THE SINGER, 56, WED THE EVENT PRODUCER, 48, IN New York City, the effect was more eerie spectacle than holy sacrament. "The church was talked about as if it were a theater," said Bob Mackie, who designed Minnelli's empire-style wedding gown and sparkly red reception dress. "It was 'backstage' and 'You cue me!'" Among the 850 cast members—er, guests—were (in alphabetical order) Lauren Bacall, Carol Channing, Joan Collins, Kirk Douglas, Mia Farrow, David Hasselhoff, Anthony Hopkins, Michael Jackson (a co-best man with brother Tito), Gina Lollobrigida, singer Mya (who, despite having met Liza only twice in her life, was one of 13 bridesmaids), Donny Osmond, Mickey Rooney (and his eighth wife) and Elizabeth Taylor as co-matron of honor. Despite the bold-name bonanza, the groom insisted, "We really don't need anyone around us to have fun." Perhaps. But rather than risk finding out, the newlyweds negotiated their own *Osbournes*-style reality series. VH1 signed on, only to cancel the project pre-premiere due to difficulties with the prima donna duo.

divorces

Jennifer Lopez & Cris Judd

WAS THIS THE MARITAL EQUIVA-
lent of a palate-clearing sor-
bet? A little something to
refresh the appetite between the main
events: a two-year relationship with
Sean "P. Diddy" Combs and a heated
romance with Ben Affleck? Engaged
only three months after she left Combs,
Lopez married dancer Judd in a lavish
ceremony. But, echoing her short-lived
1997 union to waiter Ojani Noa, the
pair (both 32) split after a mere eight
months. They remain "extremely ami-
cable," they stated, and Judd continues
as her choreographer.

Drew Barrymore & Tom Green

I RECOMMEND PEOPLE DON'T GET IN HIGH-PROFILE marriages," said Green, 31, after his split from Barrymore, 27. "There are a lot of people in the world. You don't have to marry someone with their own team of publicists, managers, agents and lawyers." Coupling with the famous does have some advantages, however. Green had to have known all about his fiancée's well-documented first marriage (to bar owner Jeremy Thomas in 1994), which lasted less than eight weeks. Having filed for divorce after five months, Green did say gallantly, "Drew is a wonderful woman. I love her very much. I wish our marriage could have worked out." Barrymore echoed his sentiments, saying, "He has always been a great friend, and that won't change."

Jennifer & Sir Anthony Hopkins

M ARRIED WITH A BABY WHEN HE MET JENNI LYNTON IN 1969, Hopkins left his first wife and made the film production assistant his second in 1973. This time it seemed like for keeps, but in 1995 they began living apart, she in London, he in L.A. "I don't think—and I say this with great love—that it's in Tony's nature to live with somebody," said Lady Hopkins, 57. Sir Anthony, 64, agreed: "I did the best I could to live a domestic life. I simply cannot do it."

Marcy & James Gandolfini

THROUGH THE YEARS HE'S WANdered and come back," explained the jilted wife of the *Sopranos* star. "It's like a love-hate relationship." After meeting in 1995 and being married for three years, James, 40, decided that he and Marcy, 35, each deserved a love-love relationship—but with other people. Her lawyer said that Marcy, a former public relations consultant, was surprised to be served with divorce papers. But his spokesman maintains that the couple, who have a son, Michael, 2, hadn't lived together for months. "As to why," said his rep, "it's a private matter."

Lorraine Bracco & Edward James Olmos

A LEGAL SIEGE BY BRACCO'S ANGRY EX, HARVEY Keitel, seeking custody of their daughter Stella, cast a continuing cloud over her union with Olmos. The *Sopranos* shrink and the *Stand and Deliver* teacher wed in 1994, only to split in '97, according to the divorce petition Olmos finally filed in 2002. Their estrangement did not prevent Bracco, 46, and Olmos, 55, from appearing together in a 1998 remake of *The Taking of Pelham One Two Three.*

Vivica A. Fox & Christopher Harvest

DECEMBER 19 HAD BEEN AN AUSPICIOUS DAY FOR the *Soul Food* star, 37, and her R&B singer beau, 32. On that date in 1996 the two met at an L.A. club, where Harvest, who is known professionally as Sixx-Nine (for his height), bought her 20 roses. On that day in '97 he proposed in a rose-filled room, and on the second anniversary of their meeting they wed (yet more roses). But the bloom was off the rose before December 2002: Fox had filed for divorce in June.

Valerie Bertinelli & Eddie Van Halen

AS RECENTLY AS JULY 2001, THE TV star, 42, and her rocker husband, 47, cuddled at a movie premiere. But three months later they secretly split and she moved out of their home with son Wolfgang, 11. In July 2002 they made the separation public. "This is something she tried very hard not to have happen," said Bertinelli's mother. But after enduring the guitar virtuoso's repeated bouts with alcoholism and resistance to rehab, as well as his refusal to give up smoking after a diagnosis of tongue cancer (now, he says, in remission), Bertinelli had had enough. Still, they had defied doubters by hanging in for 20 years, and friends like her *One Day at a Time* sister Mackenzie Phillips predict, "They'll be close forever."

Brooke & Jeff Gordon

A TRUE "TROPHY" WIFE (THEY MET WHEN HE WON AT DAYTONA and she was the beauty handing out the loving cup), Brooke, 31, listed "marital misconduct" as her reason for leaving the NASCAR racer, 30. During their seven-year union, Jeff amassed $47 million in prize money. Thus, in making her appeal for her fair chunk of it, Brooke pointed out to the court that she had dressed him well and had made him more attractive to corporate sponsors. Moral? Never underestimate the legal prowess of a scorned raceway model.

Holly Hunter & Janusz Kaminski

S TEVEN SPIELBERG PLAYED CUPID, INTRO-ducing his *Schindler's List* cinematographer, 42, to the actress, 43, in 1994. (He was the best man at their wedding a year later.) But even the *E.T.* director's magic touch couldn't help the two Oscar winners overcome what Kaminski cited as "irreconcilable differences."

Kelly Winn & Kiefer Sutherland

SEPARATED FROM WINN, 40, SINCE 1999, Sutherland, 35, said that things went bad in their marriage when "I got more involved in *my* life than in *ours*." Before they formally ended it in 2002, their life had included an extended family of Winn's two boys and his daughter from a first marriage to actress Camelia Kath. (That was followed in 1991 by a famously short-circuited engagement to Julia Roberts.) Of late, and since his breakthrough in *24,* said a pal, "Kiefer has grown up a lot."

Roseanne & Ben Thomas

FORCED TO SHARE HER TV FORTUNE with exes Bill Pentland and Tom Arnold, Roseanne, 49, announced in 1995 before marrying Thomas, 35, her former bodyguard, "Honey, there'll be prenuptial agreements up the ying-yang from henceforth." She trotted out hers with Ben during a brief 1998 split (they symbolically re-wed on her talk show) and had it handy when she asked for a divorce in 2002.

Victoria Gotti & Carmine Agnello

IS THERE NO FAMILY LOYALTY IN the Mafia anymore? With her husband, 41, a scrap-metal dealer in prison on racketeering and tax-evasion charges, the author (and scion of late Mob boss John Gotti), 39, ended their 17-year union. They have three children.

Nikki & Ian Ziering

HIS IS WHO IAN WANTED—THE BLONDE BOMBSHELL," REPORTED a friend of the former *90210* denizen, 37. What he didn't want, said the pal, was someone so "focused on herself." So after four years he left Nikki, 30, a *Price Is Right* model and former *Playboy* Playmate. The day after he filed for divorce (but before it was made public), Nikki was judging a beauty pageant alongside Dr. Joyce Brothers, who noted, "She was more cheerful than she should be. She was covering up."

Monica & Mike Tyson

AN IT POSSIBLY END WELL WHEN YOU court your future husband while he's serving a sentence for rape? Not in this case. After five years of marriage and two kids, Monica, 35, a pediatrics resident in Washington, D.C., left the former heavyweight boxing champ, also 35, charging adultery.

Vanna White & George Santopietro

WE'LL SEE HOW IT GOES," SAID *Wheel of Fortune*'s White, 45, back in December 2001, when the couple announced a trial separation. Unfortunately, their time apart went well enough for the game show fixture and her restaurateur husband, 56, to end their 11-year marriage. Ever ebullient, White said, "The truth is we're great friends," and requested joint custody of their children, Nicholas, 8, and Giovanna, 4.

Tawny Kitaen & Chuck Finley

FOUR DAYS AFTER SHE WAS CHARGED with spousal abuse for allegedly kicking veteran baseball pitcher Finley, 39, with her stiletto heels while he was driving, actress Kitaen, 40, became the respondent in their divorce suit. A married couple for four years, they have two daughters, Wynter, 9, and Raine, 3.

Melissa Rivers & John Endicott

NINE YEARS IS A LONG TIME," said Rivers, 34, defending the end of her relationship with the horse trainer. They were wed (in a glitzy event impresarioed by her mother and E! cohost, Joan) for four years and had a son, 1, when Endicott, 36, filed for divorce, citing irreconcilable differences.

births

MARCH 2002

Angelina Jolie

THE ONLY MAN IN MY LIFE RIGHT now is Maddox," Jolie, 27, said in September 2002. What a difference a few months made. In March, she and Billy Bob Thornton, 47, were notorious for wearing vials of one another's blood around their necks and seemed as obsessively together as ever when they adopted a son, born in Cambodia the previous summer. Though the adoption was delayed briefly as the U.S. government investigated allegations of baby selling there, soon they were rejoicing as a family. "He's cute as hell!" bragged Thornton, who has three other kids (and four prior marriages). Grandpa Jon Voight volunteered, "I'm very good at changing diapers!" By summer, however, Jolie had filed for divorce, and court papers revealed that the adoption certificate contains only her name. Evidently the actress had grown estranged from her father too, as he turned up on *Access Hollywood,* weepily pleading for her to seek help for her "serious mental problems." Jolie, who legally dropped "Voight" from her name but kept "Thornton" in her son's, countered that she is in fine fettle, as is Maddox. At his first birthday party, a guest pointed out that the child "was very happy playing with his cake but was only interested in eating his broccoli."

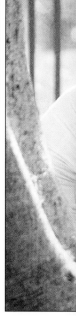

Uma Thurman & Ethan Hawke

MOST HUSBANDS, HOWEVER SENsitive, don't have a clue what their wives go through during pregnancy. Actor-novelist Hawke, 31, at least made an effort toward empathy by writing part of his 2002 book *Ash Wednesday* from the point of view of a very gravid female narrator. His research was no doubt aided by watching his wife, Thurman, also 31, carry daughter Maya Ray, 4, and more recently their new son, Roan Green. Despite such attentiveness, Hawke admits that he isn't always the perfect husband and father. In order to find peace to write, he confessed, "I try to get out of the house before my kids wake up."

Christine Taylor & Ben Stiller

WHEN ELLA OLIVIA MADE FIRST-TIME grandparents of Jerry Stiller and Anne Meara, the delighted grandpa mused, "I need to have another child of my own." At 75, he might leave the procreation to his son, 36, and daughter-in-law, 30. (The *Zoolander* costars married in 2000.) With so many cutups in the family, the senior Stiller added, "I worry that if I start telling her jokes, she is liable to say to me, 'I already heard that one from Daddy.'"

JULY 1, 2002

Janet Holden & Eric McCormack

I WOULD LOVE HIM TO BE A MUSICIAN, SPEAK EIGHT LANGUAGES, be a zoologist, play great jazz piano—all the stuff I was too lazy to do," said McCormack, 39, of Finnigan, the first child born to the *Will & Grace* lead and his director wife, 36. For early musical training, Dad says he vocalizes around the house "bad '70s songs and musical theater. I'm hoping to get into his brain and really pervert it, in a good way."

MARCH 2, 2002

Anne Heche & Coleman Laffoon

HOMER HECHE LAFFOON WAS NAMED FOR his paternal grandma, whose nickname honored her storytelling skills. Sadly, his mom's storytelling in her memoir *Call Me Crazy* kept her own family away after his birth. (The book alleges that Heche's late father abused her.) With her cameraman husband, 28, the actress, 32, said her current goal was to become "a boring mommy and a boring wife."

Josie Bissett & Rob Estes

BACKSTABBING, GIRL FIGHTS, SEXUAL MUSICAL CHAIRS: *Melrose Place* wasn't the family-friendliest environment. But since it fell off the TV road map in 1999, two of the show's stars have settled into real-life domesticity. Married before *Melrose,* Estes, 38, and Bissett, 31, became parents in 1999 with son Mason Tru. Then in 2002 they added a daughter, Maya. (Mason reportedly tracked his sister's development, placing a pacifier on his mother's navel toward the end of the pregnancy.) The soap-star-turned-Neutrogena-pitchwoman has so taken to her new life that she is promoting a line of toys on a kids' Web site. "Shifting my focus felt natural," said Bissett, "because I'm so passionate about being a mom."

Elizabeth Hurley

THE ARRIVAL OF BABY DAMIAN Charles was met by a "radiant" mother, reported a friend, in a room "overloaded with more flowers than a hothouse." And by controversy. A single mom, the *Austin Powers* star, 36, named her former lover Stephen Bing, an American movie producer, as the father. But Bing, 37, who was also the subject of another paternity suit, claimed the couple weren't exclusive and doubted the baby could be his. Bollocks, said Hurley, as did the press in her native London, which dubbed her ex the "love rat." Eventually a DNA test provided corroboration, clearing Hurley's name and making Damian a possible claimant to Bing's $600 million fortune. Surrounded by supportive friends, Hurley christened her son at 3 months. Former flame Hugh Grant was one of six godfathers.

APRIL 9, 2002

Vanessa Paradis & Johnny Depp

THE INEVITABILITY OF FATHERHOOD has always affected the film choices I've made," said the actor, 38, not long after his son Jack John Christopher Depp III was born in Neuilly, France. "From *Cry Baby* to *Edward Scissorhands* . . . I did them with the idea that I would ultimately be able to leave them for someone." He and girlfriend Paradis, 29, a French-born singer, already had one heir to the Depp film canon, daughter Lily-Rose Melody, 2.

MARCH 18, 2002

Juliette Norton & Jamie Oliver

ENGLAND'S NAKED CHEF AND HIS wife, both 26, welcomed daughter Poppy Honey in March. But by autumn, Norton, a model, was craving lamb with mint sauce, as well as Thai Bites rice crackers and Marmite (a fermented yeast spread). The Food Network star recognized her unusual menu requests as a sign of early pregnancy, and his Web site soon confirmed that Jools had another bun in the oven, due to arrive in the spring of 2003.

SEPTEMBER 1, 2002

Victoria & David Beckham

ROMEO'S GORGEOUS! HE'S GOT Brooklyn's nose and Victoria's chin," reported the smitten father, 27, a superstar on England's Manchester United soccer team, of his second son with the Spice Girl formerly known as Posh, 28. (Their marriage is as hallowed in their home country as a union between Tiger Woods and Britney Spears might be here.) Romeo joined brother Brooklyn, 3, after a cesarean birth scheduled not to fall on one of Beckham's match days.

APRIL 11, 2002

Julianne Moore & Bart Freundlich

ONE OF THE INDUSTRY'S BUSIEST ACTRESSES, Moore, who appeared in four 2001 films and had two more (*The Hours* and *Far from Heaven*) ready for Christmas, 2002, slowed down considerably after giving birth to daughter Liv. With son Caleb just 5, she decided, "I had to take a solid year off." But Moore, 42, who lives with the kids' father, director Freundlich, 32, didn't worry about dropping off Hollywood's radar. At 5 months, Liv jetted off with the family to the Venice Film Festival. Judges there praised Moore's *Heaven* performance, but she was focused mainly on her daughter, asking reporters, "Isn't she just beautiful?"

ON WITH THE SHOWS
Friends' Jennifer Aniston (right) thrilled at her first victory. Winner's-circle vet Denzel Washington showed Halle Berry (opposite) the ropes. MTV host Jimmy Fallon (below right) sent up Eminem's video persona—or was it Burt Ward? And a gold gramophone went out to the girls of the new "Lady Marmalade" (below), who performed with the song's originator, Patti LaBelle.

■ the grammys

■ the video music awards

Hollywood's
Big Nig

hts

After passing a somber time, the famous were ready to dress up, party and, yes, laugh again. Hosts Whoopi, Jon, Jimmy and Conan obliged, and giggles could be heard between recitations of that all-important phrase, 'And the winner is . . .'

The Oscars

- **BEST PICTURE**
  A Beautiful Mind

- **BEST DIRECTOR**
  Ron Howard,
  A Beautiful Mind

- **BEST ACTRESS**
  Halle Berry,
  Monster's Ball

- **BEST ACTOR**
  Denzel Washington,
  Training Day

- **BEST SUPPORTING ACTRESS**
  Jennifer Connelly,
  A Beautiful Mind

- **BEST SUPPORTING ACTOR**
  Jim Broadbent,
  Iris

- **BEST ORIGINAL SCREENPLAY**
  Julian Fellowes,
  Gosford Park

- **BEST ADAPTED SCREENPLAY**
  Akiva Goldsman,
  A Beautiful Mind

- **BEST FOREIGN LANGUAGE FILM**
  No Man's Land

- **BEST SCORE**
  Howard Shore,
  Lord of the Rings

- **BEST SONG**
  Randy Newman,
  "If I Didn't Have You,"
  Monsters, Inc.

HALLE BERRY
"God, just don't let me embarrass my mother," Berry (in an Elie Saab gown) admitted to thinking when she accepted the first Best Actress Oscar given to an African-American.

JENNIFER LOPEZ
Wrapped in pink Versace, Lopez won raves for her taste in clothes but drew snide comments for what designer Randolph Duke called her "Barbarella hair."

JENNIFER CONNELLY
The *Beautiful Mind* star, in Balenciaga, came prepared to win. Having already snagged the Golden Globe, she mounted the stage with a polished thank-you speech on a crib sheet.

JULIA ROBERTS
"I love my life!" shouted 2001's Best Actress (in a jersey Armani dress) as she breathlessly presented her pal and *Pelican Brief* costar Denzel Washington with an Oscar (his second).

GWYNETH PALTROW
Topping everyone's "what were they thinking?" list, the otherwise reliably elegant presenter had slouched down the red carpet trussed up in a see-through Alexander McQueen creation.

The Emmys

54th Annual Emmy Awards
PRESENTED SEPTEMBER 22, 2002

- DRAMA SERIES
  The West Wing

- COMEDY SERIES
  Friends

- ACTRESS, DRAMA
  Allison Janney,
  The West Wing

- ACTOR, DRAMA
  Michael Chiklis,
  The Shield

- ACTRESS, COMEDY
  Jennifer Aniston,
  Friends

- ACTOR, COMEDY
  Ray Romano,
  Everybody Loves Raymond

- SUPPORTING ACTRESS, DRAMA
  Stockard Channing,
  The West Wing

- SUPPORTING ACTOR, DRAMA
  John Spencer,
  The West Wing

- SUPPORTING ACTRESS, COMEDY
  Doris Roberts,
  Everybody Loves Raymond

- SUPPORTING ACTOR, COMEDY
  Brad Garrett,
  Everybody Loves Raymond

- MINISERIES
  Band of Brothers

- MADE-FOR-TV MOVIE
  The Gathering Storm

JENNIFER ANISTON & BRAD PITT
What a night for Mrs. Pitt! After nine seasons, *Friends* finally took top comedy honors, she earned her own Emmy, and her husband, who had sported the Grizzly Adams look all year, cleaned up for the occasion.

OPRAH WINFREY

"What a great honor, being alive and fitting into this dress," cheered the daytime diva (in Bradley Bayou) after receiving the first Bob Hope Humanitarian Award from Tom Hanks.

KIM CATTRALL

The *Sex and the City* nominee, who e-mailed her absent, pregnant costar Sarah Jessica Parker during the ceremony, tried 14 other outfits before settling on this Hervé Léger gown.

STOCKARD CHANNING

The *West Wing* winner (in a Richard Tyler design) capped the evening with a second Emmy for her portrayal of Matthew Shepard's mother in the TV movie about the slain gay man.

The Grammys

44th Annual Grammy Awards
PRESENTED FEBRUARY 27, 2002

- **RECORD OF THE YEAR**
"Walk On," U2

- **ALBUM OF THE YEAR**
O Brother, Where Art Thou?
Soundtrack, various artists

- **SONG OF THE YEAR**
"Fallin'," Alicia Keys

- **POP VOCAL, FEMALE**
"I'm Like a Bird,"
Nelly Furtado

- **POP VOCAL, MALE**
"Don't Let Me Be Lonely
Tonight," James Taylor

- **POP VOCAL, GROUP**
"Stuck in a Moment You
Can't Get Out Of," U2

- **R&B ALBUM**
Songs in A Minor,
Alicia Keys

- **COUNTRY ALBUM**
*Timeless—Hank Williams
Tribute,* various artists

- **RAP ALBUM**
Stankonia, OutKast

- **ROCK ALBUM**
*All That You Can't Leave
Behind,* U2

- **POP VOCAL ALBUM**
Lover's Rock, Sade

- **BEST NEW ARTIST**
Alicia Keys

DESTINY'S CHILD
Before dispersing for solo projects, Beyoncé Knowles, Kelly Rowland and Michelle Williams (from left) showed up in Versace to perform with Alejandro Sanz and pick up a best R&B group award for "Survivor."

NELLY

No. 1, at least to his jeweler, the artist born Cornell Haynes Jr. was runner-up to Missy Elliott. Her "Get Ur Freak On" trounced Nelly's "Ride wit Me" in the solo rap category.

CELINE DION

Having returned from her self-imposed family leave, the Canadian chanteuse looked like 100 million bucks—her reported salary for a three-year gig in Las Vegas—in Christian Dior.

SHERYL CROW

Although she has chided younger pop stars for selling their sound with skimpy clothes, Crow justified this Henry Duarte number by saying, "Turning 40 agrees with me. I'm busting out."

MTV Awards

CHRISTINA AGUILERA
Perhaps to promote her new single "Dirrty"—or to bury her Mouseketeer past—the singer wore practically nothing to present a Moonman to her nemesis, Eminem.

AVRIL LAVIGNE
"Dude," intoned the evening's best new artist, "this is amazing. I've had this dream for a very long time." The 17-year-old Canadian pop star wore her now standard tank top and necktie.

BRITNEY SPEARS
Split from 'N Sync's Justin Timberlake, who sang solo during the show, Spears—not a girl, not yet a dominatrix—dressed to ensure she'd get her share of the attention too.

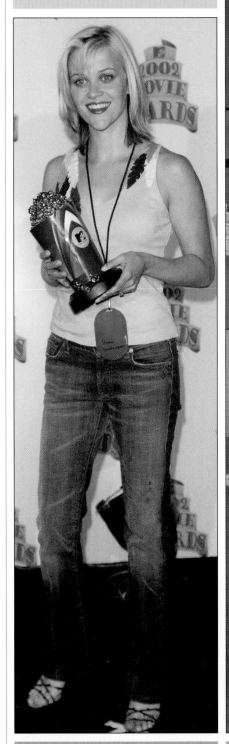

REESE WITHERSPOON
Comfortable in her element—her hit *Legally Blonde* had three nominations and earned her best comedy performance honors—the sometime glamor girl showed up in blue jeans.

BRITTANY MURPHY
A presenter, Murphy backed up host Jack Black during the show-opening audience sing-along and later gave Eminem, her *8 Mile* costar, a friendly bird during his number.

VIN DIESEL
The newly minted action star lost in the best male performance category to Will Smith of *Ali* but shared a win for best onscreen team with *Fast and the Furious* buddy Paul Walker.

8th Annual Screen Actors Guild Awards
PRESENTED MARCH 10, 2002

37th Academy of Country Music Awards
PRESENTED MAY 22, 2002

PATRICIA HEATON
"I've never worn iridescent fuchsia before," beamed the *Everybody Loves Raymond* star, in Thierry Mugler. Getting nominated was another first, but she lost to Megan Mullally.

DEBRA MESSING
"Debra wanted to go edgier," said her stylist, and did with a Gucci hook-and-eye dress and Brian Atwood shoes. Remarkably, the *Will & Grace* star declared the outfit "comfortable."

LEE ANN WOMACK
The Texas native, nominated for top female vocalist, paired with Willie Nelson to sing "Mendocino County Line." A Dallas paper called the intergenerational duet "warm, if a bit weathered."

59th Annual Golden Globe Awards
PRESENTED JANUARY 20, 2002

KENNY CHESNEY
A onetime marketing undergrad, nominee Chesney launched his country career with hits like "She Thinks My Tractor's Sexy." Sure, but what does she think of the puka shell/cowboy hat combo?

JENNIFER GARNER
"It's kind of been all about the dress," said the *Alias* star of her preshow anxiety. The sheath was by Vera Wang, who also gowned Garner for her wedding to *Felicity* actor Scott Foley.

NICOLE KIDMAN
A winner for her singing turn in *Moulin Rouge*, Kidman sparkled in a gown by Tom Ford for Yves Saint Laurent Rive Gauche. Fellow Aussies Russell Crowe and Judy Davis also won Globes.

c.1926

1940

1961

Tributes

We mourn royalty also in the realms of laughter, song and personal advice, bidding farewell to Milton Berle, Dudley Moore, Rosemary Clooney, Peggy Lee, Ann Landers and others

ROYALTY

Elizabeth, the Queen Mother

SHE SEEMED GLORIOUSLY UNSTOPPABLE," said Prince Charles of his grandmother. Indeed, at age 98 she twisted the night away at the wedding of Prince Edward and Sophie Rhys-Jones. Born to Scottish nobility, Elizabeth Angela Marguerite Bowes-Lyon was soon known as the best dancer in the London debutante whirl. Flirtatious and popular, she rejected the original proposals of her pal Bertie but wed him in 1923 and became Queen Consort 14 years later when he was crowned King George VI. Painfully shy and stammering, George shrewdly relied on Elizabeth's charisma, and they were worshipped by wartime Britons for their courageous decision to remain with their two young daughters, Elizabeth and Margaret, in England (at Windsor Castle), even as Buckingham Palace was bombed. "The children could not leave without me, I could not leave without the King, and the King will never leave," she explained. When he died in 1952 and was succeeded by their older daughter, she became Queen Mother. Through the decades of divorce and Diana, she was easily the best-loved royal, maintaining an exhausting public schedule until her death at 101. She also played the ponies, went fly-fishing and enjoyed raising a glass of gin—and she only left the dance floor at Edward's wedding when the Queen herself said, "Come on, Mummy, it's time for bed."

ACTOR

Dudley Moore

IF I'D BEEN ABLE TO HIT SOMEONE IN THE NOSE, I WOULDN'T have been a comic," he once said. Had he grown past 5'2", we might not have known his humor or impish charm. Bullied as a kid, Moore compensated with outsize talent. A classically trained pianist, he won a music scholarship to Oxford. But wit proved a more effective weapon, and Moore plied it to early success with Cambridge pal Peter Cook in *Beyond the Fringe,* a comedy revue that stormed Broadway in the early '60s. In 1979 he romped with Bo Derek through *10,* and in 1981 brought delicious abandon to his breakout role as the incorrigibly lovable millionaire in *Arthur.* Known in the tabs as Cuddly Dudley, he had at last found acceptance as a short, shaggy sex symbol, romancing towering girlfriends like 5'11" actress Susan Anton. Moore died at 66 from complications of a neurological ailment that had left him unable to walk, talk or play his beloved piano. But, as he proved when someone told a joke at a party for him last year, Moore could still deliver a laugh. The sound, said one attendee, "made everyone around the table almost weep with joy."

DIRECTOR
Billy Wilder

IT WAS RIGHT OUT OF A BILLY WILDER MOVIE. AN ASPIRING SCREENWRITER helps out his prostitute neighbor by hiding her client in his apartment when her raging boyfriend comes home. The client turns out to be a studio exec, so the young man thrusts a script into his hand. "I'll buy it," says the grateful film honcho. "Feels like a good story." So Samuel Wilder busted his way into the movies, first in Berlin, then in Hollywood when Hitler's invasion forced the exodus of some 1,500 film artists. (Wilder's mother and stepfather perished in Auschwitz.) One of the very few who overcame the language barrier to thrive in American cinema, Wilder had an ear for sharp dialogue that distinguished some 50 films that genre-jumped from comedy (*Some Like It Hot,* above, with Jack Lemmon in drag) to melodrama (*Sunset Boulevard*) to noir (*Double Indemnity*). Offscreen he was as biting as his most venomous characters. "You have Van Gogh's ear for music," he told one actor. He earned 21 Oscar nominations (and won six), and when showered with what he called "quick-before-they-croak" awards before his death at 95, Wilder said he would trade them all for the chance to make one more movie.

SINGER

Rosemary Clooney

THOUGH NEVER A FAN OF SILLY songs, Clooney built her career with fluff like 1951's "Come On-a My House." She got her start performing at rallies for her grandfather's mayoral campaigns in Maysville, Kentucky, and soon sang, said director Mike Nichols, "like Spencer Tracy acts." An actress as well (her brother Nick is George Clooney's father), she costarred with Bing Crosby in *White Christmas* and married actor José Ferrer, with whom she had five children. But Ferrer, she said, broke her heart "in small increments" with his cheating. Their final breakup in 1967, coupled with witnessing the assassination of her friend Robert Kennedy, sent Clooney to an L.A. psychiatric ward for a month. Back on the jazz and cabaret circuit in the '90s, she did the Mercer, Porter and Gershwin songbooks. But someone would inevitably request "How Much Is That Doggie in the Window?"—a Patti Page novelty. Said a bemused Clooney, who died at 74 from lung cancer: "They probably figure if it's a bad song, I must have done it."

ACTOR

Robert Urich

WHILE MANY ACTORS SEE TELEVISION AS A STEPPING STONE to movie stardom, Urich seemed right at home on the small screen. In fact, he holds the record for starring in the most series (15), beginning with a TV version of *Bob & Carol & Ted & Alice* in 1973 and ending with 2001's *Emeril,* a sitcom featuring the celebrity chef. But Urich, a self-described "uptight Catholic boy" raised in an Ohio steel town, made his name playing no-nonsense sleuths on *Vega$* and *Spenser: For Hire.* Married to Heather Menzies, who portrayed Louisa in *The Sound of Music,* Urich developed a rare cancer of the joints in 1996 and died at 55. On one of his last TV appearances he was a celebrity contestant on *Who Wants to Be a Millionaire,* raising money for cancer research.

ACTOR
Rod Steiger

BARREL-CHESTED AND OWL-faced, Steiger reconciled himself early to his lack of leading-man looks and went on to embody an impressive range of characters, from the lovesick Italian-American butcher in *Marty* to the corrupt New York lawyer in *On the Waterfront* to the Russian cad in *Doctor Zhivago*. After a tour as a torpedoman in World War II, Steiger joined a local theater group in Newark, New Jersey, in the hopes of meeting women. Later the G.I. Bill would pay for a drama degree in New York City. His study with Lee Strasberg served him well—he won an Oscar for *In the Heat of the Night*—but he was rarely lucky in love. Divorced four times, he finally found happiness with actress Joan Benedict in 2000. Afflicted with clinical depression in the '80s, Steiger attempted suicide three times but later controlled the disease and crusaded for mental health research. Never having been a heartthrob, Steiger, who died at 77 after intestinal surgery, didn't worry about aging onscreen. "The mechanism may get old," he said of his craft, "but the sense of poetry never dies."

Larry Rivers

JAZZ SAX PLAYER RIVERS FELL INTO modern art after reading a book on the subject and wound up helping to revolutionize it. At a time when abstract expressionists like Jackson Pollock dominated, Rivers brought back the human form, not to mention humor, making way for the irony of pop artists like Andy Warhol. An upstart in the field, Yitzroch Loiza Grossberg (as he was born) infuriated Pollock, who, he said, "once tried to run down one of my sculptures" with his car. Rivers was a natural draftsman ("He can do anything he wants with a brush," said *The New York Times*) and self-promoter. He appeared in films, on a quiz show and around New York on his motorcycle before his death from cancer at 78. A Renaissance man who divided critics, Rivers "would stab out at different things, like Picasso did," said gallery owner friend David Levy. "Except that more of Picasso's things worked out."

John Entwistle

FOR YEARS, NOBODY EVEN NOTICED JOHN WAS THERE," joked Pete Townshend about his bandmate. Nicknamed the Ox, Entwistle, The Who's stoic bassist, could get overlooked next to the guitar-smashing Townshend and gale-force vocalist Roger Daltrey. But from The Who's 1964 start, he was as integral as his flashier cohorts. He wrote darkly humorous hits like "Boris the Spider," and his bass lines provided the ballast for the others' frenetic performances. A sometime artist, he did the caricatures of the band that appeared on the cover of *The Who by Numbers*. On the eve of a 2002 reunion tour, Entwistle died at 57 of an apparently cocaine-induced heart attack in his hotel room. Still in mourning, the band played on.

ACTRESS/WRITER

Carrie Hamilton

WAS ALWAYS CAROL BURNETT'S daughter," said Hamilton in 1979 at age 15. "When I got high, I wasn't anymore." A Hollywood scion (dad was Joe Hamilton, who produced Burnett's comedy series), Carrie fell into a typical trap of unearned fame and privilege: She became a teenage drug addict. But unlike those whose similar stories end tragically, Hamilton worked hard to kick cocaine and psychedelic drugs and, with her mother, publicized the risk of substance abuse to the young. They spoke unflinchingly about how her addiction hurt the family (the Hamiltons divorced in 1984) and traveled to Moscow to help open the first Russian branch of Alcoholics Anonymous. Sober, she forged an entertainment career out of her mother's shadow. A role on TV's *Fame* led to her starring in the 1988 film *Tokyo Pop,* for which she received excellent notices. She earned a directing award for one of her two short films and in the '90s led a touring company of the Broadway hit *Rent.* Recently she had cowritten a play with Burnett, *Hollywood Arms,* based on her mother's memoir. A smoker since her teens, Hamilton succumbed to lung cancer at 38, just months before its Broadway premiere.

ADVICE COLUMNIST

Ann Landers

BORN TO RUSSIAN IMMIGRANTS IN SIOUX CITY, IOWA, 17 MINUTES BEFORE her twin, Pauline Esther, Esther Pauline Friedman was also first to launch an advice column. In 1955 she became Ann Landers for the *Chicago Sun-Times* and brought in her sister to help open mail. Soon Pauline got a rival gig as Dear Abby, and the twins, while helping to heal others' family rifts, did not speak for years. But with tens of millions of devotees between them, Landers and her sister reconciled, recognizing, said Abby, "there's more than enough for both of us." Wed (in a 1939 double ceremony with Pauline) to Budget Rent A Car tycoon Jules Lederer, she had a daughter, Margo Howard (now an online advice dispenser for *Slate*), but divorced after 36 years. Famous for telling her readers—whose letters she often read in the tub—to "wake up and smell the coffee," Landers, who died at 83 of multiple myeloma, said of her own marriage, "The lady with all the answers does not know the answer to this one."

BALLPLAYER

Ted Williams

HE STOOD OUT LIKE A WHITE COW IN A PASTURE OF BROWN COWS," SAID the Boston Red Sox official who recruited the sleek, 6'3" San Diegan in 1938. Three seasons later the Splendid Splinter hit .406, the last player ever to clear .400. His career slugging stats might also have been unequaled if he hadn't served five years as a pilot in World War II and Korea. Even the egotistical Joe DiMaggio once conceded, "I always felt like I was two steps behind him." Teddy Ballgame, as he was known, let his work speak for itself, stiffing sports reporters and refusing to tip his cap in acknowledgment of the ovations that hailed his homers. But Boston fans forgave and loved this patriot and philanthropist who raised enormous funds for childhood cancer research. When he died at 83 (he was born just 12 days before the last time the Sox won the World Series), the Fenway Park announcer proclaimed, "There goes the greatest hitter who ever lived."

John Gotti

THE "TEFLON DON" OF NEW YORK City tabloids, Gotti headed the nation's most powerful organized crime syndicate for seven years, taunting unsuccessful prosecutors by cavorting at the city's best Italian restaurants in $2,000 Brioni suits, even as he insisted that he earned $60,000 a year dealing in plumbing supplies. In fact, he had earned his last honest dollar as a teen working in garment factories and later hauled in an estimated $10 million plus per annum from Mob activities. A protégé of Gambino mafioso Aniello Dellacroce, Gotti took control of the family in a bloody 1985 power play and, unlike most camera-shy underworld figures, enjoyed the celebrity of being *capo di tutti capi*. But with the help of Mob turncoat "Sammy the Bull" Gravano, the Feds finally made murder and racketeering charges stick in 1992. The Gambino clan was in decline, and Gotti was in prison in Illinois when he died of cancer at 61.

ACTOR

Josh Ryan Evans

DREAM BIG," WROTE EVANS WITH EACH AUTOGRAPH. Born with achondroplasia (a form of dwarfism) and a heart condition, Evans spent much of his childhood hospitalized, watching movies and dreaming of becoming an actor himself. Full-grown at 3'2", he realized his goal, playing a child lawyer on *Ally McBeal*, a young Grinch in *How the Grinch Stole Christmas*, and, for three years, the living doll Timmy on the supernatural soap *Passions*. But by age 20 his heart could no longer keep up with his ambitions. He died, said his mom, having done "exactly what he planned to."

ACTOR
Harold Russell

THE ONLY ACTING RUSSELL HAD done before his turn as a disabled sailor in William Wyler's *The Best Years of Our Lives* was in an army training film for disabled vets. Russell, who enlisted the day after Pearl Harbor, lost both hands in an explosion during the war. The Motion Picture Academy nominated Russell as a supporting actor but, fearing he didn't have a chance against Clifton Webb or Claude Rains, arranged for a special Oscar for "courage." Surprisingly, he also beat out Rains and the others for the real thing. Russell often joked that he was so adept at using the hooks which replaced his hands that he could pick up anything but a dinner check. With few roles available to him, Russell, who died at 88 from a heart attack, left Hollywood, started a P.R. firm and headed President Johnson's committee on Hiring the Handicapped.

REPORTER
Howard K. Smith

KNOWN FOR DELIVERING YOU-ARE-THERE DISPATCHES in a gentle Louisiana cadence, Smith started out in 1941 as one of Edward R. Murrow's "boys" covering the war in Europe. Though objective in the field, he believed journalists should "take sides on public issues." That got him fired in 1961 when, after witnessing Ku Klux Klan violence, he said on CBS that the U.S. was in danger "of becoming a racial dictatorship, like Nazi Germany." He landed at ABC and stayed until 1979. (Sam Donaldson recalls Smith, then 59, doing handstands in the studio for exercise.) Smith, who died at 87, found a second career playing reporters in films like *Network*.

Peggy Lee

THE TERM "TORCH SINGER" COULD HAVE BEEN coined for Lee—just listen to the slow, controlled burn of her signature hit, "Fever." The arrangement had called for a full orchestra until she threw it out. "What I want," she decided, "is bass and drums and finger snapping." That's all Norma Deloris Egstrom (as she was born in North Dakota) required to back her distinctive cooing, soothing vocals. She also appeared in films, notably writing and performing "The Siamese Cat Song" for Disney's *Lady and the Tramp* and earning an Oscar nod for *Pete Kelly's Blues*. Lee continued to tour and command the stage seated with a jeweled cane into the 1990s; she was 81 when she died of a heart attack. Wed four times, she insisted on being called Miss Peggy Lee. Tony Bennett preferred another title: the "female Sinatra."

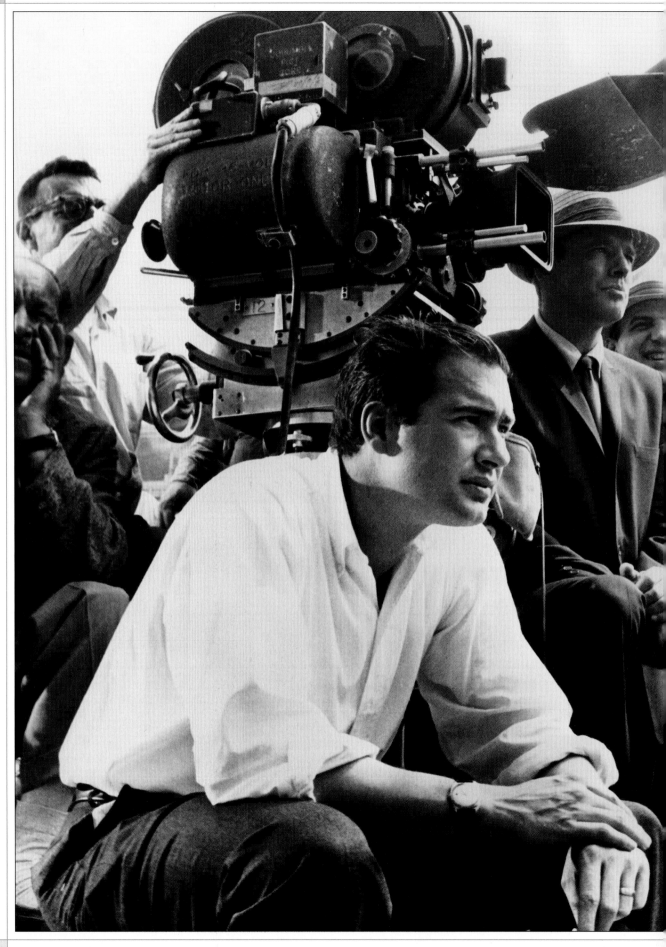

DIRECTOR
John Frankenheimer

FOR THE MOST PART HIS CHARAC-
ters are men, real men," wrote a
Los Angeles Times critic, "fight-
ing each other or some outside force
trying to destroy a way of life." Having
picked up his camera facility while
shooting Air Force movies during the
Korean War, Frankenheimer came to
Hollywood with a gift for artfully
telling stories of morality and justice.
In 1962 alone, he released both the
political thriller *The Manchurian
Candidate* and *Birdman of Alcatraz*.
He made his name first, however, in
television, directing 152 live dramas
for *Playhouse 90* and other anthology
series between 1954 and 1960. By the
time he was 30 he had earned five of his
14 Emmy nominations. In the 1970s
Frankenheimer's work suffered from
his alcoholism. He made poor film
choices and received few offers. For a
while he disappeared to France to study
cooking at Le Cordon Bleu. After kicking his drinking habit, he was welcomed back into television, recently
directing critically praised TV movies
like *George Wallace* and 2002's *Path
to War*. He died at 72 from a stroke
following spinal surgery. Of his varied
work, live drama was his favorite: "We
had the final cut, and you had no such
thing as a difficult actor."

DESIGNER
Pauline Trigère

PARIS-BORN TO RUSSIAN PARENTS, SHE GREW UP TO BE A QUINTESSEN-
tial American designer. "This country made me Pauline Trigère,"
said the Seventh Avenue doyenne, whose reversible coats, back-
less jumpsuits and seemingly seamless dresses adorned society women
for five decades. World War II had forced her to leave France with her
husband, with whom she started her business. The pair were headed
to Chile, but a New York stopover changed her mind. In 1961 she made
fashion history by putting the first African-American model on the
runway. A master tailor—she could cut a coat from draped fabric
without ever touching a sketch pad—Trigère was also her own best
model and never stepped out in anyone else's clothes. A stickler for
detail, she left instructions that after her death (which came at 93) she
should be cremated wearing red lipstick. "What does it matter? Who
will know?" asked a friend. Replied Trigère: "I'll know."

ACTRESS
Kim Hunter

HUNTER, A BROADWAY STAR AND Oscar-winning actress, cared more for craft than for kudos. She let her kids use the Oscar she won for her portrayal of Stella Kowalski in 1951's *A Streetcar Named Desire* as a target in games of ringtoss. A Detroit native, Hunter was as at ease onstage in New York City (where she originated the part of Stella in 1947) as she was on a soundstage in a monkey suit playing Dr. Zira, the simian psychiatrist in *Planet of the Apes* (and two of its sequels). Her career suffered after *Streetcar* because Hunter was blacklisted during the McCarthy '50s. Never a member of the Communist party, she suspected she had been targeted because she had cosponsored a peace conference. Eager to work, she appeared on the soap *The Edge of Night* and was still at it in the 1997 film *Midnight in the Garden of Good and Evil.* "I thank God I'm in a profession," said Hunter, who died at 79 after a heart attack, "where there is no retirement age."

ACTOR/WRITER
Matt Robinson

A MEMBER OF *SESAME STREET*'S MULTIRACIAL FIRST CAST— a distinction that got it banned briefly in Mississippi following its 1969 premiere—Robinson helped make TV history. He originated the role of Gordon, a human neighbor to the *Street*'s Muppet denizens, and voiced the purple-faced puppet Roosevelt Franklin. Two actors have played Gordon since he left in 1971 to write films, Cosby scripts and plays, including *The Confessions of Stepin Fetchit,* based on his conversations with one of Hollywood's first black movie stars. The father of actress Holly Robinson Peete, he died at 65 from Parkinson's disease.

Chuck Jones

A SMALL CHILD ONCE SAID TO ME, 'YOU DON'T DRAW Bugs Bunny, you draw pictures of Bugs Bunny.'" Jones loved that little boy's accusation, because, he said, "it means that he thinks the characters are alive, which, as far as I am concerned, is true." Also alive within Jones were, among others, Porky Pig, Daffy Duck, Elmer Fudd and Acme catalog addict Wile E. Coyote. Beginning as a cartoon cel cleaner in 1932, Jones rose through the ranks of the Warner Bros. animation studio to direct 300 films—including *Dr. Seuss's How the Grinch Stole Christmas*—and to win three Oscars. His last picture, before his death at 89, was a final go-round for the Coyote and the Road Runner called *Chariots of Fur.* But the character with whom he most identified was Daffy, said his wife, Marian. "He said he screwed up like Daffy all the time. He'd rather be Bugs. But Bugs was too much of a hero."

DIRECTOR

Ted Demme

HE COULD HAVE TRADED ON HIS famous name or just worked for Uncle Jonathan. (The elder Demme directed the Oscar-winning *Silence of the Lambs.*) Instead, Ted, a native New Yorker, chose to make his own way in the business, starting as a production assistant at MTV and eventually helping to create the *Yo! MTV Raps* series. Demme then directed a series of memorable ads for the channel featuring the rantings of an un-known comic named Denis Leary. The spots launched both their careers and made them fast friends whose many collaborations included the 1994 film *The Ref.* Two years later the bittersweet high school reunion comedy *Beautiful Girls* established Demme as a fine director in his own right. More importantly, friends and colleagues knew him as a fine person. "There was nobody who didn't like Teddy," said screenwriter Nick Cassavetes, who worked with Demme on *Blow,* the 2001 movie about American cocaine kingpin George Jung. The father of two small children, Demme died suddenly of a heart attack at 38 while playing in a celebrity basketball game.

SUPREME COURT JUSTICE

Byron R. White

WHIZZER" WHITE WAS, AND IS LIKELY TO REMAIN, THE ONLY PERSON to both lead the NFL in rushing (twice) and to serve 31 years on the Supreme Court (the fourth-longest tenure). Getting there was a balancing act. He deferred a 1938 Rhodes scholarship to play pro ball, then after military service he took a break from Yale Law School to join the Detroit Lions. In 1962 President Kennedy, his Navy pal, appointed White to the high court. Though a Democrat, the Colorado native cast some surprisingly conservative votes, among them a dissent in 1973's *Roe v. Wade,* which legalized abortion. But he was strictly antisegregationist and in favor of free expression, voting to strike down a law banning strip clubs. Try as he could to put his sports-hero image behind him, White remained an athlete under the robes, taking on his law clerks at basketball in the Supreme Court gym into his 60s. He died at 84 of pneumonia.

PORN STAR TURNED REFORMER
Linda Lovelace

FOR TWO DECADES, LINDA BOREman was a uniquely qualified antipornography crusader: As Linda Lovelace, she had starred in 1972 in the first mainstream X-rated movie, *Deep Throat.* The film earned more than $600 million and became a cultural landmark—its title became the alias for the key Watergate informant—but Boreman (her birth name) claimed that the movie, in effect, depicted her rape. She shot it, she said, under threat of violence by her then manager husband. (Before divorcing him in 1973, she appeared in a sequel.) She later wed a construction worker and became a mother and grandmother. Appearing with feminist heavyweights Gloria Steinem and Catherine MacKinnon, she frequently spoke about the porn industry's oppression of women. Still, Boreman would also drop in at memorabilia shows and screened *Deep Throat* not long before her death at 53 in a car accident. Her reported reaction to the film? "I don't see what the big deal was."

ACTRESS
LaWanda Page

THE PERFECT CANTANKEROUS FOIL FOR REDD FOXX'S junkman in *Sanford and Son,* Page's Aunt Esther held her own with the show's free-flying insults, like "Nice having her around—makes the junk look so pretty." In reality, Foxx and Page were childhood friends who played the same comedy clubs on the "chitlin' circuit" before their 1970s sitcom earned top ratings. An Ohio native, she entered show business as a dancer and flame swallower called "The Bronze Goddess of Fire." Late in life, Page played several more TV roles in the crusty image of Esther before her death from diabetes at 81.

Dave Thomas

DON'T CUT CORNERS," INSTRUCTED HIS GRAND-mother, who helped raise Thomas after the death of his adoptive mother. So in 1969, when he opened the first Wendy's fast-food outlet in Columbus, Ohio, he listened to Grandma and made the burgers square. A high school dropout, Thomas started in food service at 15 and earned his first million by age 35 as a Kentucky Fried Chicken franchisee. He then grew his own business (named after one of his daughters) into a chain with annual sales of $6 billion. Famous for starring in some 800 commercials to promote Wendy's, he was a generous supporter of adoption, including those by single parents and gay or interracial couples. "I say, 'Hey, fine—as long as it works for the child,'" he said. Nine years before his death at age 69 from liver cancer, Thomas finally earned his high school diploma—and took wife Lorraine to the prom.

Ruth Handler

HER IDEA WAS TO MAKE A PLAYTHING FOR her daughter, not to become a lightning rod for feminist criticism. Young Barbara Handler liked dressing grown-up-looking paper dolls in fashionable clothes, and Mom wondered why she couldn't have a fleshed-out doll with real clothes. The child's resulting namesake became one of the world's bestselling toys. But Barbie's top-heavy figure (39-21-33 if she were 5'6") caused critics to accuse the dollmaker of disturbing little girls' body image. In truth, Handler was a woman most feminists could embrace. An entrepreneur when most wives stayed home, she founded toymaker Mattel with her husband, Elliot, and partner Harold Mattson and introduced its most popular line. Today there are more than a billion Barbies worldwide. (Her devoted plastic boyfriend is named for Handler's son Ken.) In 1970 Handler was diagnosed with breast cancer. (She died at 85, following colon surgery.) A mastectomy led her to a new calling: designing prosthetics for other cancer survivors, including former First Lady Betty Ford. "I've lived my life," Handler once quipped, "from breast to breast."

John Weitz

ONE OF HIS FAVORITE QUOTES FROM SHAKESPEARE WENT, "ONE MAN IN his time plays many parts." Weitz did, amassing a CV that included intelligence officer, fashion designer, novelist, historian and recreational auto racer. An émigré from Berlin, Weitz returned to Germany in 1944 with the OSS (precursor of the CIA). Ten years later in New York City, he presided over a clothing label known for its practical sportswear (he favored crease-resistant suits). A licensing pioneer, he reaped a fortune putting his name on socks, ties and cologne in deals that would continue posthumously. "My presence, you see," he noted, "is not exactly necessary." His books included a biography of Hitler's foreign minister, a guide to men's grooming and manners, and two novels. Married twice (the second time to actress Susan Kohner), Weitz, who died at 79 from cancer, was the father of four, including the codirectors of *American Pie*, Paul and Christopher Weitz.

Johnny Unitas

IT'S LIKE BEING IN A HUDDLE WITH God," his teammate John Mackey once said. For 18 years (17 with the Baltimore Colts) Unitas graced the NFL with unearthly talent and authority. Preceding today's rock-star, prime-time quarterbacks, this crew-cut, true-grit, blue-collar athlete was generally agreed upon to be the greatest ever to play the position. But it was a long slog. He made his Pittsburgh high school team only when another quarterback was injured. Notre Dame rejected him, and he wound up at the University of Louisville. Not picked until the ninth round of the 1955 NFL draft, he was soon dropped by the Pittsburgh Steelers and forced to take a construction job. Then the Colts ventured a $7,000-a-year contract, which he rewarded with three league championships (and three MVP honors). Unitas paid for his lengthy career in a battering line of work. His hand was so weakened, for example, that he required Velcro to hold a golf club. A twice-married father of eight, he died at 69, after a heart attack. "He had a real hunger," recalled former Colts coach Weeb Ewbank. "This was a kid who wanted success and didn't have it for so long that he wasn't about to waste it when it came."

MAKEUP ARTIST

Kevyn Aucoin

HE FULFILLED IN THE FACES OF WOMEN THEIR FONDEST DREAMS FOR themselves," said photographer Irving Penn. Aucoin did so with simple tools: foundation, powder, lipstick. Even during the over-the-top '80s he favored the natural look—using cosmetics to make it look as though none were used—which remains the dominant trend. A Max Factor for our celebrity-obsessed era, Aucoin (pictured with model Linda Evangelista) soon commanded up to $6,000 a day and reflected the glow of the luminaries he painted, from Julia Roberts and Gwyneth Paltrow to Barbra Streisand. Raised in Louisiana, he used his proximity to fame to promote gay rights as well as racial and physical diversity in fashion. Aucoin, who died at 40 from a brain tumor, once told a reporter, "If all it says on my gravestone is 'Did Good Lipstick,' I'd rather it say nothing at all."

Lisa Lopes

AN EQUAL THIRD OF TLC, THE bestselling female group in pop history, "Left Eye" Lopes inadvertently found solo fame in 1994 when she set fire to the Atlanta mansion of boyfriend Andre Rison, a professional football player. Though no one was hurt, the law took her arson seriously, sentencing her to five years probation and a $10,000 fine. While contrite, Lopes also saw the incendiary lovers' spat and its resulting media coverage as a way to boost TLC's profile. She and fellow members Tionne "T-Boz" Watkins and Rozonda "Chilli" Thomas posed on the cover of a magazine in firefighter gear. That attitude—coupled with the two singers' deep and velvety voices and Lopes's staccato raps—eventually helped move 11 million copies of *CrazySexyCool,* released in the wake of the controversy. Fans embraced TLC and "Left Eye" (the nickname was given by a boyfriend who believed one of her eyes was bigger than the other) for their catchy singles about deadbeat suitors ("No Scrubs"), AIDS ("Waterfalls") and self-esteem ("Unpretty"). The Philadelphia-born daughter of an amateur musician who, she said, abused both her and her mother, Lopes had found peace in recent years by meditating at a retreat in Honduras, where she had purchased three nearby acres to build a camp for impoverished children. Traveling there with a start-up girl group she was mentoring, Lopes was killed in a car accident at age 30. Her bandmates plan to continue as a duo. Said Thomas: "You can't replace a TLC girl."

Bill Blass

FANS, AMONG THEM NANCY REAGAN AND GLORIA VANDERBILT, CALLED him Mr. Right. (Anne Klein, an early employer, wasn't so sure. She fired him for having "good manners but no talent.") Under his own label, begun in 1960, Blass offered women casual elegance, as, for instance, a ball gown paired with a sweater set. But taste alone does not build an empire. The Indiana-born son of a dressmaker and hardware store owner began putting his logo on the outside of garments in 1968 and thus became one of the first celebrity designers. He was also among the first to license his name for other products, anointing everything from chocolates to automobiles (but wisely turning down caskets). Up until he sold his firm for $50 million in 1999, Blass logged thousands of miles attending department store trunk shows, a rarity among fashion royalty. At these appearances, Blass, who died at 79 from throat cancer, was said to "charm the clothes right onto a woman's back."

MUSICIAN
Lionel Hampton

IALWAYS LIKED TO BE TAKING BOWS," HE SAID, AND HAMP HAD A LOT OF opportunities, having begun thwacking away on the xylophone in his teens in the 1920s and continuing to tour nearly until his death at age 94. Born in Louisville, Kentucky, Hampton honed his talent with a band in his grandmother's Alabama church and at a music school founded by a black Chicago newspaper for its newsboys. A trailblazer on the vibraphone, he also broke racial barriers by playing with Benny Goodman's orchestra before forming his own in 1940. The group was a training ground for such future jazz greats as Charlie Mingus, Dinah Washington, Dexter Gordon and a 15-year-old Quincy Jones. (Hampton's wife soon sent the youngster back to school.) Said Jones of his mentor: "He taught me how to groove and how to laugh and how to hang and how to live like a man."

ROYALTY
Princess Margaret

DISOBEDIENCE IS MY JOY," SHE famously said. But the Queen's little sister did not disobey on the one occasion when it might have brought her lasting happiness. Forbidden to marry the divorced Royal Air Force captain Peter Townsend, Margaret broke off their romance in 1955 and later wed the marginally more acceptable photographer Antony Armstrong-Jones. (While he posed no affront to the Anglican Church, Armstrong-Jones was not the nobleman the court had in mind.) After 18 years and two children, the couple divorced, ushering in the era of Windsor sunderings and scandals after 400 years of dutifully intact marriages. She never re-wed but had several relationships which occasionally grabbed headlines—once when some love letters were inadvertently made public and years later when photos turned up of Margaret sunbathing with a naked boyfriend. Though she had little patience for carrying out royal tasks like cutting ribbons or christening ships, Margaret did revel in the lifestyle her title afforded her. She held her own informal court of celebrities like Elizabeth Taylor and Mick Jagger, often at her winter villa on the Caribbean isle of Mustique. Remembered fondly as a party girl rarely without her tortoiseshell cigarette holder or a drink, the Princess died at 71 after a series of strokes.

MUSICIAN
Waylon Jennings

"WE GOT LONGHAIRED PEOPLE, LAWYERS, DOCTORS and all the cowboys," Jennings said of his audience. He attracted them with what he and pal Willie Nelson called the "outlaw" sound, which threw off country music's formulaic shackles. Fans rewarded him with 16 No. 1 hits, eight gold records and country's first solo platinum album, *Ol' Waylon* (1977). By the 1990s his image had mellowed—he had kicked a drug habit and released a children's CD. Still, Jennings, who died at 64 from diabetes, had a few surprises left for Nashville, as in 1996 when he joined heavy metal acts like Metallica on rock's Lollapalooza tour.

GOLFER
Sam Snead

IN 1937, JUST THREE YEARS AFTER buying his first set of golf clubs—the story goes that he had trained as a kid by hitting rocks with branches—Snead won his first PGA event. It wasn't long before the self-taught Virginian became a sensation, as known for his coconut straw hat and down-home chatter ("Now stay put, you little fooler, this ain't gonna hurt none at all," he'd tell the ball) as for his picture-perfect swing. In 1950 he set the record for most wins (11) in a season (Tiger Woods's best is nine), and he eventually racked up 81 PGA titles, including three Masters. In addition to the spoils of six decades on the links, Snead, 89, earned plenty more endorsing golf clubs, headache powders, deodorants and a motel chain bearing his name. Yet he was widely known for his Depression-era thrift, advising folks to "keep close count of your nickels and dimes, stay away from whiskey, and never concede a putt."

DIRECTOR
Bruce Paltrow

THOUGH LESS PUBLICLY KNOWN THAN HIS DAUGHTER Gwyneth or wife, Blythe Danner, Paltrow was an influential TV director and producer. Two of his series—*The White Shadow*, about a high school basketball team, and *St. Elsewhere,* set in an urban hospital—paved the way for ensemble workplace dramas like *ER* and *NYPD Blue* (which his son Jake directs). Cast with promising young stars (Denzel Washington, Helen Hunt), his shows broke ground with issue-driven stories: *St. Elsewhere* had an HIV-positive character in 1983. He also respected reality—students on *Shadow* eventually graduated. Paltrow, who died at 58 from pneumonia following a recurrence of throat cancer, once said that his and Danner's careers kept them from their kids more than they would have liked. In 2000 he managed to harmonize work and family by directing Gwyneth in the film *Duets*.

RAP PIONEER
Jason Mizell

OUR BEATLES," IS HOW PUBLIC Enemy's Chuck D explained Run-DMC. You couldn't overstate the influence of rap's first platinum group. Behind the turntables on '80s hits like "My Adidas" and the Aerosmith collaboration "Walk This Way" was DJ Jam Master Jay, as Mizell was known, laying down scratches and beats that showed generations of hip-hop artists how to do it. (Lest anyone question who was responsible for the provocative new sounds, Jay made himself the subject of many good-natured, self-congratulatory raps, and the group disbanded upon his death.) Raised in a middle-class neighborhood in Queens, New York, the members of Run-DMC (Rev. Joseph "Run" Simmons and Darryl "DMC" McDaniels are the others) created music with a social conscience—Jay insisted on one song about staying in school. As gangsta rap took over the genre, they became elder statesmen, refusing to write violent lyrics to stay with the times. So it was especially tragic when Mizell, a husband and a father of three sons, died at 37 from a gunshot to his head, fired by an unknown assailant. Unlike their hip-hop heirs, said Simmons, "Jay was more about trying to help."

ACTOR

Jonathan Harris

LOST IN SPACE*'S* EVIL BUT INEPT DR. ZACHARY SMITH DELIVERED his trademark barbs ("Bumbling bag of bolts," he called Robot, above) in an English accent. Asked if he was British, the actor born Jonathan Charasuchin to Russian-Jewish parents in the Bronx answered, "No, just affected." Raised on trips to the Yiddish theater, he spent his early career on the Broadway stage, once appearing opposite Marlon Brando in *A Flag Is Born.* But it was the scheming doctor, forever stranded aboard the Robinson family's spaceship, that made him famous in the 1960s. Harris, married for 64 years to wife Gertrude, with whom he had one son, died at 87 from a blood clot in his heart. Just months before, he had recalled his *Lost in Space* days as "the most fun in the whole world. I loved creating that dreadful, wonderful man."

Paul Wellstone

A DECENT, GENUINE GUY WHO had a different philosophy from almost everyone else," is how former Republican Senator Bob Dole recalled his colleague. While campaigning to represent Minnesota for a third term, Wellstone, 58, died in a plane crash, along with his wife, Sheila, also 58, daughter Marcia, 33, three aides and two pilots. (His death opened the door for the Republicans to regain Senate control when his replacement, former Vice President Walter Mondale, lost to Norm Coleman.) Diagnosed in January with multiple sclerosis, Wellstone, a school wrestling champ and popular ex-college professor, was an energetic figure on the Senate floor. Leaping to his feet to argue passionately on behalf of farmers, union members and the poor, he was often the odd man out in 99-1 votes—and the only Democrat up for reelection to oppose President Bush's Iraqi war resolution. Survived by two sons and six grandchildren, Wellstone would always instruct kids, "Don't be cynical. If there are things you think should be changed, become part of making it happen."

James Coburn

I'VE BEEN DOING THIS WORK FOR OVER HALF MY LIFE. I finally got one right, I guess," said Coburn when he picked up his first Oscar, for a 1998 role as Nick Nolte's abusive father in *Affliction.* Known for creating memorable villains—from the ruthless knife-throwing Britt in 1960's *The Magnificent Seven* to the spidery CEO Henry J. Waternoose in 2001's *Monsters, Inc.*—Coburn also put his sly smile to work in two '60s Bond send-ups, *Our Man Flint* and *In Like Flint.* Married twice and the father of two, Coburn lost years of work in the 1980s to crippling arthritis. After conquering the pain of the disease, he resumed filmmaking with a vengeance. "Actors are boring when they're not working," he once said. *The Man from Elysian Fields* and *American Gun* were headed for the cineplexes when he died in his wife's arms at 74 of a heart attack.

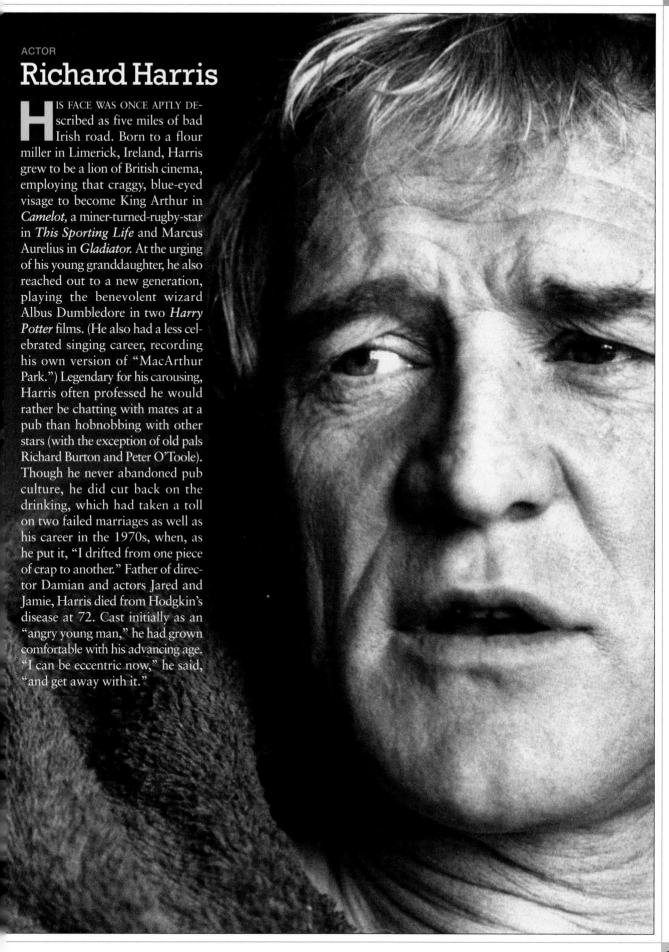

Richard Harris

HIS FACE WAS ONCE APTLY DEscribed as five miles of bad Irish road. Born to a flour miller in Limerick, Ireland, Harris grew to be a lion of British cinema, employing that craggy, blue-eyed visage to become King Arthur in *Camelot,* a miner-turned-rugby-star in *This Sporting Life* and Marcus Aurelius in *Gladiator.* At the urging of his young granddaughter, he also reached out to a new generation, playing the benevolent wizard Albus Dumbledore in two *Harry Potter* films. (He also had a less celebrated singing career, recording his own version of "MacArthur Park.") Legendary for his carousing, Harris often professed he would rather be chatting with mates at a pub than hobnobbing with other stars (with the exception of old pals Richard Burton and Peter O'Toole). Though he never abandoned pub culture, he did cut back on the drinking, which had taken a toll on two failed marriages as well as his career in the 1970s, when, as he put it, "I drifted from one piece of crap to another." Father of director Damian and actors Jared and Jamie, Harris died from Hodgkin's disease at 72. Cast initially as an "angry young man," he had grown comfortable with his advancing age. "I can be eccentric now," he said, "and get away with it."

TV PIONEER

Milton Berle

MR. TELEVISION MADE HIS TV DEBUT TO APPROXIMATELY 12 PEOPLE, HE SAID (it was in 1929). Six decades later, when he received an Emmy nomination for playing an Alzheimer's patient on *Beverly Hills, 90210,* more Americans had TV than had indoor plumbing, a fact attributable, in part, to Berle himself. After the 1948 premiere of his *Texaco Star Theater,* Uncle Miltie made the new-fangled boxes a national necessity. His effect on the civilization was astounding. Other shows, but not his, were canceled for coverage of the Truman-Dewey election. Nightclubs closed on Tuesdays when he was on. He caused a water shortage once in Detroit when nearly every household simultaneously flushed at 9:05 p.m., after the show ended. Thrust into vaudeville at age 10 by a mom who, he joked, "made Gypsy Rose Lee's look like Mother Teresa," Berle was a club and radio star when he took on television. He invented the variety show, right down to the applause sign. A playboy who dated preacher Aimee Semple McPherson, Marilyn Monroe and Lucille Ball, he was married four times to three women. The father of two children—and a nation of couch potatoes—died at 93.

NEWLY AFFIANCED costars Jen and Ben said goodbye to the past and faced their future together, while . . .

. . . OLD MARRIEDS Jen and Brad savored her success.